T121 CB D

e Open
University

first level
disciplinary
course

using Mathematics

BLOCK D
MODELLING UNCERTAINTY

Computer Book D

Prepared by the course team

'UTER BOOK

D

About this course

This computer book forms part of the course MST121 *Using Mathematics*. This course and the courses MU120 *Open Mathematics* and MS221 *Exploring Mathematics* provide a flexible means of entry to university-level mathematics. Further details may be obtained from the address below.

MST121 uses several software packages, including Mathcad (MathSoft, Inc.), to investigate mathematical and statistical concepts and as a tool in problem solving. All the software packages are provided as part of the course. Their use is covered in the four computer books, of which this is one.

The Open University, Walton Hall, Milton Keynes, MK7 6AA.

First published 1997. Reprinted 1997

Copyright © 1997 The Open University

Edited, designed and typeset by the Open University using the Open University TEX System.

Printed in the United Kingdom by Caligraving Limited, Thetford, Norfolk.

ISBN 0 7492 7816 1

This text forms part of an Open University First Level Course. If you would like a copy of *Studying with The Open University*, please write to the Course Enquiries Data Service, PO Box 625, Dane Road, Milton Keynes, MK1 1TY. If you have not already enrolled on the Course and would like to buy this or other Open University material, please write to Open University Educational Enterprises Ltd, 12 Cofferidge Close, Stony Stratford, Milton Keynes, MK11 1BY, United Kingdom.

1.2

Contents

Guidance notes

This computer book contains those sections of the chapters in Block D which require you to use your computer. Each of those chapters contains instructions as to when you should first refer to particular material in this computer book, so you are advised not to work on the activities here until you have reached the appropriate points in the chapters.

For advice on how each computer session fits into suggested study patterns, refer to the Study guides in the relevant chapters. The statistical software for Block D needs to be installed on your computer. This block does not draw on Mathcad.

Installing the statistics software

The software for Block D is contained on two disks, labelled MST121 Using Mathematics Block D, Disk 1 and Disk 2. To install the software, follow the instructions below (for *Windows 3.1* or *Windows 95*, as appropriate).

Windows 3.1

◇   Insert Disk 1 into drive A.

◇   Choose **Run** from the **File** menu of Program Manager.

◇   Type **a:\setup** in the box which appears, and click on the OK button.

◇   Follow the instructions on the screen.

The installation will set up a Program group window named **MST121 Block D** containing four icons, named **Simulations**, **CLT**, **OUStats** and **StatsAid**.

Windows 95

◇   Insert Disk 1 into drive A.

◇   Choose **Run** from the **Start** menu.

◇   Type **a:\setup** in the box which appears, and click on the OK button.

◇   Follow the instructions on the screen.

The installation will set up a window containing four icons, named **Simulations**, **CLT**, **OUStats** and **StatsAid**. Close this window now.

The Windows 95 Taskbar

When you first start to learn about multi-tasking, you will find it easier to track what applications you have running if the Taskbar is always visible or, in technical terms, 'always on top'. However, if you have a standard 640×480 resolution display, there will be times when setting the Taskbar 'always on top' will obscure part of an application that you wish to see.

We recommend that when you are using the statistics software, you set the Taskbar such that it is *not* 'always on top'. To do this

◇   right-click on the Taskbar;

◇   from the pop-up menu select Properties;

◇   select the tabbed dialogue box marked Taskbar options;

◇   ensure the box 'always on top' is not checked.

About the software

The software for Block D has four components: *Simulations, OUStats for MST121, StatsAid* and *CLT.* You will be using *Simulations* in Chapters D1 and D3. The main component of the software is *OUStats for MST121,* which will be referred to in this book simply as OUStats; this is a data analysis package and will be introduced in Chapter D2 and used in each of the remaining chapters of the block.

StatsAid is a computer-mediated learning (CML) package designed to support Block D of MST121. It explains most of the statistical prerequisites of the course, covering some of the statistical topics taught in the course MU120, and contains exercises on each topic included. How you decide to use this package is up to you – you may choose to work through each of the topics covered or only some of them, or you may choose not to use the package at all. The six topics covered are as follows.

> Frequency diagrams
> The median and quartiles
> Boxplots
> The mean
> Standard deviation
> Scatterplots

In this block, it is assumed that you are familiar with each of these topics. Frequency diagrams are needed from the start – they are used in Section 1 of Chapter D1. The mean is first mentioned in Section 4 of Chapter D1; and the standard deviation and scatterplots are used in Chapter D2 (in Sections 2 and 4, respectively). The median, quartiles and boxplots are used in Chapter D4 after being reviewed briefly in Section 1 of that chapter. If you are unsure of any of these topics, then you may find it helpful to work through the appropriate sections of *StatsAid* before you meet them again in the text.

You will find instructions for using *StatsAid* in Appendix 3 of this computer book.

The software *CLT* was used in the video band associated with Chapter D3; you will not be required to use it in this block, but it has been included so that if you wish to you can explore further the ideas discussed in the video band. Its style is similar to that of *Simulations,* so no separate instructions for its use are included in this computer book.

If you have not already done so, install the software for Block D on your computer.

The first activity takes you through some of the basic features of the probability simulations which are provided as part of the statistics software.

Activity 2.1 Probability simulations

(a) *Windows 3.1*: Double-click with the mouse on the **Simulations** icon in the **MST121 Block D** window.

Windows 95: Click on the **Start** menu, move the mouse pointer to **Programs**, then to **MST121 Block D** and click on **Simulations**.

The remaining instructions are the same whether you are using *Windows 3.1* or *Windows 95*.

Click again with the mouse, and you should see a menu containing the following options.

> Experiments
> Settling down
> Heads
> Waiting for a success
> Collecting a complete set
> Confidence intervals
> Exit

In this section, you will be using all the simulations except the last; you will use Confidence intervals in Chapter D3.

If at any time you wish to return to the desktop, click on **Exit**.

(b) A simulation can be opened by clicking on its button using the mouse. Click on **Experiments** to open this simulation, and you should see the screen shown in Figure 2.1.

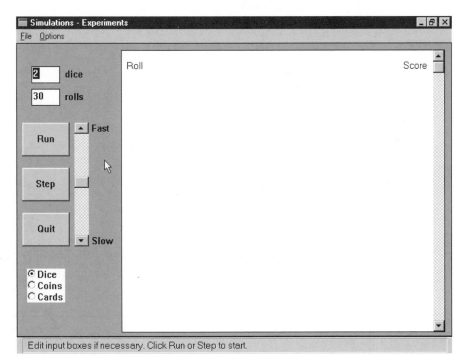

Figure 2.1 The opening screen for the **Experiments** simulation

This screen was produced using *Windows 95*. There is no major difference between screens produced by *Windows 95* and those produced by *Windows 3.1*.

At the bottom left of the screen are three radio buttons labelled **Dice**, **Coins** and **Cards**. The default option is **Dice**. A different option can be selected either by clicking on its name (**Coins** or **Cards**) or by clicking on its button.

Select **Coins**.

Now enter the following settings in the boxes at the top left of the screen.

    1 coins

   30 tosses

The procedure for doing this is explained below, in case you are not sure how to do it.

You will notice that when the option **Coins** is selected, you are provided with default values for the number of coins and the number of tosses; these values are 2 and 30, respectively. Notice also that the number 2 is highlighted.

There are two ways of changing the default settings. First, you can change a number which is highlighted simply by typing in a new number; the old number is replaced with the number you type in. Try typing in a different value for the number of coins now. Notice that your new number is not highlighted. To highlight this number, double-click on it. In general, double-clicking in a box highlights the number it contains.

Clicking once in a box removes a highlight and positions the cursor in the box. A number which is not highlighted can be edited using the cursor keys, the Delete key and the Backspace key.

Try changing the number of coins several times, to familiarise yourself with these two methods.

You can move the cursor to another box by clicking in the box. Alternatively, if you press the Tab key, the cursor will move to the next box on the screen (in this case, the box for the number of tosses) and the number it contains will then be highlighted. This number can be overtyped or edited as described above. Try doing this now.

Now change the settings to 1 coin and 30 tosses.

If you press the Tab key repeatedly, the cursor selects each of the boxes or buttons in turn. Try this now. You can make use of this feature to run the simulation, or to quit, without using the mouse. For example, if the option marked **Run** is selected in this way, then confirming it by pressing **Enter** will run the simulation. However, it is simpler to run the simulation by clicking on **Run**. Do this now.

Follow the outcomes of 30 tosses of a coin as they appear on the screen. Once the simulation is completed, you can use the scroll-bar (on the right of the screen) to scroll back through the outcomes.

(c) Two features of the simulation that we have not yet mentioned are the speed slider, which is located to the right of the **Run** and **Quit** buttons, and the **Step/Pause** button. By dragging the speed slider with the mouse, the speed of the simulation can be altered. (Note that dragging a screen object involves placing the mouse pointer on the object and then moving the mouse while holding down the mouse button.) Try running the simulation once more and, while it is running, adjust the speed using the slider. First slow it down, then speed it up.

Situated below the **Run** button is a button labelled **Step**. Each time **Step** is clicked, one toss of a coin is simulated. Click **Step** several times now to see the effect.

Next, click **Run** and set the speed to slow using the speed slider. Notice that the **Step** button is now labelled **Pause**. Click on **Pause**: the simulation is interrupted. (Whenever the **Pause** button is clicked, the simulation currently in progress is interrupted.) Notice that you can continue the simulation either by clicking **Run** or by clicking **Step**.

Spend a few moments exploring these facilities.

If nothing happens when you click on **Dice** or **Cards**, then check that your previous simulation has finished and is not still running slowly or 'paused'.

(d) Now explore the options **Dice** and **Cards**. When you have finished using this simulation (or indeed any of the simulations), you can return to the probability simulations menu by clicking on **Quit**. When you have finished exploring the options, click on **Quit**.

You have now explored the first computer simulation. Before going on to use the second one, it is worth reflecting on the art of designing a 'good' computer simulation. On the one hand, a software designer will wish to exploit the power of the computer in order to reduce repetitive routine calculations and tasks, and present only a distilled summary of the reality being simulated. On the other hand, if what you see on the screen differs too much from this reality (the repeated tossing of coins, or whatever), the result can seem abstract and confusing.

The simulation which you have just run is intended as a sort of halfway house between reality and abstraction. It has the advantage of remaining close to the real-world activity of tossing coins, but it fails to exploit the computer fully. The remaining simulations, which are explored in the following activities, exploit the computer more effectively, although the particular situation being simulated may not always be obvious from the screen. As you work through the activities which follow, make sure that you understand what each simulation represents.

Activity 2.2 invites you to use the **Settling down** simulation to explore the 'settling down' phenomenon observed in Activity 1.1 of Chapter D1.

Activity 2.2   Settling down

(a) Open the simulation **Settling down** and you will see the screen shown in Figure 2.2.

The commands in the **Options** menu allow you to choose **Thick lines** for this simulation and, using **Tones**, to have sound with the simulation.

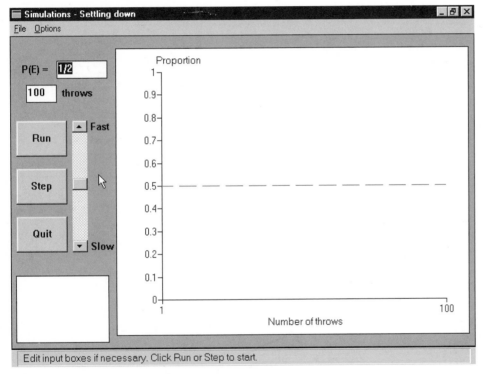

Figure 2.2   The opening screen for the **Settling down** simulation

(b) The default number of throws is 100. Reset the number of throws to 30. Now click **Step** and observe the outcome in the bottom left part of the screen. Notice how the result is displayed on the graph. Click on **Step** several times, checking as you do this how the graph corresponds to the data at each step. The simulation is 'doing' what you did with a real coin in Activity 1.1 of Chapter D1.

If you now click **Run** to complete the simulation, the graph will be completed. Note that at any time you can alter the speed at which the simulation runs (by dragging the speed slider). You can also interrupt the simulation and step through it at any point during its run (by clicking **Pause** and then **Step**). Thereafter, you can return to **Run** at any time.

(c) Now increase the number of throws to 100, and run the simulation once more. Run the simulation for 500 throws and then for 1000 throws. Is the settling down effect apparent in your simulations?

Comment

We cannot predict precisely the results of your simulations. However, it is likely that the settling down effect did become more marked as the number of throws increased.

Activity 2.3   The Brains Trust

Dr Joad defined the law of averages as follows:

> if you spin a coin a hundred times, it will come down heads fifty times, and tails fifty times.

The simulation **Heads** can be used to simulate tossing one or more coins up to 1000 times. The maximum number of coins allowed by the simulation is 20. Use this simulation to investigate the number of heads obtained when one coin is tossed 100 times. Then read the comment below.

Comment

Throughout this computer book, 'I' refers to a particular member of the course team who carried out these activities. The results reported have no special status, but can be used to provide a counterpoint to what you found, as well as enabling discussion of specific points that arise from her particular data.

Here is how I investigated Dr Joad's statement. Using the simulation **Heads**, I entered the following settings.

    [1] coins
    [100] tosses

Then I ran the simulation.

Two options, 'Show proportions' and 'Show frequencies', are displayed on the vertical axis at the completion of a simulation. When 'Show frequencies' is selected, the frequency is displayed at the top of each bar on the graph. When 'Show proportions' is selected, proportions are displayed. (To select an option, click on its button.)

For my simulation, the frequency displayed on the '1 head' bar was 44. When I selected 'Show proportions', the proportion of tosses which resulted in a head was displayed: this was 0.44.

I ran the simulation a further nine times, and each time noted the frequency on the '1 head' bar. The ten frequencies were as follows.

    44   49   51   48   55   46   53   46   45   52

None of my ten simulations produced exactly 50 heads, which appears to knock Dr Joad's definition firmly on the head! However, the average number of heads obtained in these ten runs is 48.9, which is quite close to 50. So the average proportion of tosses which resulted in a head was close to $\frac{1}{2}$.

Perhaps Dr Joad's definition of the law of averages could be reworded as follows:

> if you spin a coin a large number of times, the proportion of spins that result in a head will be approximately $\frac{1}{2}$.

Activity 2.4   D'Alembert's heads

D'Alembert argued that, in two tosses of a coin, there are three possible outcomes – heads on the first toss, heads on the second toss, and heads on neither toss. By his reasoning, since two of these three give at least one head, the probability that the coin lands heads at least once is $\frac{2}{3}$.

(a) Use the **Heads** simulation to investigate d'Alembert's conclusion. This time two coins are being tossed, so set the number of coins to 2. You may need to run the simulation several times, with various different numbers of tosses, in order to reach a conclusion. Record your results in a table like the one below, and write down your conclusions.

Remember that, for our purposes, tossing two coins is equivalent to tossing one coin twice.

Run	Number of tosses	Tosses which gave at least 1 head	
		Number	Proportion
1	100		
2			
3			
⋮			

(b) Do you think that d'Alembert's conjectured probability of $\frac{2}{3}$ is correct? If not, having carried out some simulations, what do you think the correct value of the probability is? Do the results of your simulations agree with the ideas you jotted down in Subsection 1.3 of Chapter D1?

Comment

We shall return to this problem in Section 3 of the main text.

Activity 2.5   Waiting for a six

In some board games, players can join in only when they roll a six with a die. In Subsection 1.3, you were invited to write down your ideas concerning several questions about the length of time (measured as the number of rolls of a die) that a player has to wait to join in a game. The simulation **Waiting for a success** can be used to investigate these questions.

(a) Open the simulation **Waiting for a success**. Each time a die is rolled, the probability of obtaining a six is $\frac{1}{6}$. If we regard obtaining a six as a success, then $P(\text{success}) = \frac{1}{6}$. The number of times the die has to be rolled to obtain a six (a success) is the wait. On the screen, enter the following values for the settings: $P(\text{success}) = 1/6$ and 1 wait.

Run the simulation several times, and try to get a sense of what lengths of wait, typically, tend to occur.

(b) Now set the number of waits to 50, and step through the first few waits to ensure that you understand what is going on. Then click **Run** to complete the simulation. You should obtain output similar to that shown on the screen in Figure 2.3.

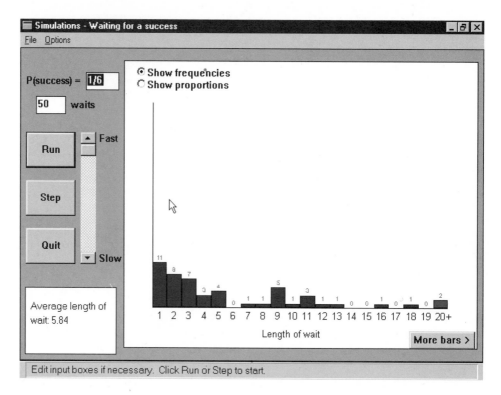

Figure 2.3 The results of a run of the **Waiting for a success** simulation

First, notice that if, as in the simulation depicted in Figure 2.3, you obtained some waits that were longer than 20, then a **More bars** button will have appeared at the bottom right corner of your screen. Clicking on this button reveals the details of these waits.

Notice also the information that appears at the end of a simulation in the box in the bottom left part of the screen. This is the average length of the waits in the simulation just run.

(c) Run the simulation several times. Can you tell from your simulation when you are most likely to achieve a six? That is, what number of rolls is most likely to be needed to obtain a six?

Comment

Overall, you may have found that your results were very variable and it was difficult to draw any firm conclusions based on just 50 waits. A greater number of waits is clearly necessary. You are asked to try this in the next activity.

Activity 2.6   Still waiting for a six

In this activity, you are invited to continue your investigation from Activity 2.5 by running the simulation a number of times for a larger number of waits. As you do so, focus on the following questions.

◇ On average, how many times will a player have to roll a die in order to obtain a six?

◇ What is the most likely number of rolls needed to obtain a six?

You may find it helpful to record your results in a table like the one below.

Number of waits	Average wait	Most likely number of rolls
300		
300		
300		
⋮		

(a) Run the simulation several times using 300 waits. On each occasion, note the average length of the waits and the number of rolls (that is, the length of wait) which occurred most frequently. What do you notice about the frequencies of the different wait lengths? How would you describe the general shape of the frequency diagram?

(b) Use your results to make hypotheses about the answers to the two questions above. Experiment with different numbers of waits to help you do this.

(c) How do your hypotheses compare with your intuitions? Were you surprised by any of the results you obtained?

Comment

The problem *Waiting for a six* is investigated further in Section 4 of the main text.

Activity 2.7   How long is an average wait?

The **Waiting for a success** simulation can be used to investigate the waiting time for other events; for example, the number of tosses of a coin needed to obtain a head, or the number of children a couple might need to have to produce a girl. If we assume that $P(\text{head}) = \frac{1}{2}$ and $P(\text{girl}) = \frac{1}{2}$, then in both examples we can use the simulation with $P(\text{success}) = \frac{1}{2}$. Other events would require different values of $P(\text{success})$.

(a) Use the simulation to explore the average wait for various values of $P(\text{success})$. Note down your results, and use them to predict a value for the average wait for each value of $P(\text{success})$ that you choose. You may find it helpful to record your results in a table like the following one.

$P(\text{success})$	Number of waits	Average wait: observed values	Average wait: prediction
$\frac{1}{6}$			
$\frac{1}{2}$			
$\frac{1}{5}$			
0.4			
⋮			

(b) Can you spot any pattern in your results? If $P(\text{success}) = p$, what would your conjecture be for the average wait?

Comment

We shall return to this problem in Section 4 of the main text.

The final two computer activities in this section use the simulation **Collecting a complete set**. It has been designed to allow you to investigate the problem *Collecting a complete set of musicians.*

Activity 2.8   Collecting a complete set of musicians

One out of eight different toy musicians is given away in each packet of a popular breakfast cereal. In Subsection 1.3 of Chapter D1, you were asked to guess the number of packets of cereal that you might expect to have to buy in order to collect a complete set of eight musicians. In this activity, you are invited to investigate this problem using the simulation **Collecting a complete set**.

(a) If necessary, change the number of objects in a set to 8 and the number of collections to 1. To make sure that you understand what this simulation does, step through the simulation until you obtain a complete set. At each step, each object has an equal chance of being selected. Objects are selected until at least one of each different type has been chosen. Notice that the number of the last object selected is highlighted on the horizontal axis. The number of objects needed to complete the collection is displayed in the box in the bottom left-hand corner of the screen.

If you run the simulation for a number of collections greater than 1, then, when the simulation finishes, all the results are recorded in the box in the bottom left-hand corner of the screen. The number of objects needed to complete each collection is displayed in the box in the bottom left-hand corner of the screen, under the heading 'Packets'. If the results are not all visible, then they can be viewed by scrolling through them. If you click on a collection number in this box, then the corresponding diagram is displayed on the screen.

(b) Now run the simulation several times, each time noting the number of packets required to obtain a complete set. Run the simulation so as to obtain at least 10 collections; write down the number of packets that were required for each simulation. (You will need to refer to your results again in Section 5 of the main text.)

Number of packets required to collect a complete set										

(c) Did you find your results surprising? Are they consistent with the ideas you noted in Subsection 1.3? Do you wish to revise the conjecture you made in Subsection 1.3 for the average number of packets required to collect a complete set? If so, then make a note of your revised prediction.

Comment

What you might have found striking was the great variability in the number of packets needed to collect a complete set of eight musicians. In Section 5 of the main text, we return to the problem of finding the average number of packets required.

Activity 2.9 Collecting a complete set

The simulation **Collecting a complete set** can be used to explore the numbers of packets needed to collect complete sets of sizes other than 8. Consider the following situations.

(a) Take a well-shuffled pack of cards, and cut the pack at random, noting the card revealed. Repeat this procedure until you have selected at least one card from each suit. How many times would you expect to have to cut the pack?

(b) You toss a coin repeatedly, noting the result (head or tail) each time. You stop at the point when you first have at least one occurrence of each outcome. How many tosses would you expect to have to make?

Explore each of these questions using the simulation **Collecting a complete set**.

Activity 2.10 Reflecting on the value of simulations

You have now investigated some problems involving chance, both physically with coins, and using computer-based simulations. In the remaining sections of this chapter, you will learn how to use probability theory to tackle these problems. But before you do this, take a few minutes now to consider what you have gained from using simulations. In particular, consider the following questions.

◇   *Intuitions*: Were your intuitions about the problems described in Subsection 1.3 reinforced by running the simulations, or were some of the results you obtained contrary to what you expected? In which problems was your intuition correct? Where, if anywhere, did your intuition let you down?

◇   *Simulation*: Do you understand what is meant by a probability simulation and how it can be used to investigate problems involving chance?

◇   *Technology*: Did you approach learning to use a new software package with confidence? Did you find running the probability simulations more or less straightforward than you expected?

Comment

The few minutes of reflection which you have just engaged in will be useful to you in several respects. First, whether or not your intuitions about chance were reinforced by your experience of running the probability simulations, you might now have a better insight into some of your preconceptions about chance. Secondly, you might have noticed from running these simulations that even where an underlying pattern exists, it can sometimes be masked by the variability in the outcomes of experiments involving chance. The outcome of an experiment involving chance, such as tossing a coin, varies from one occasion to the next, so it is difficult to see what is going on unless the experiment is repeated a very large number of times. And finally, consider whether you feel confident about using the probability simulations part of the software. If the answer is no, be prepared to spend a little time trying out some more simulations, varying the values in the boxes to see the effects.

Chapter D2
Section 3 Fitting a normal model

3.1 Introducing OUStats

In this subsection, you will be guided through some of the facilities of OUStats, the data analysis part of the statistics software. Instructions for the computer activities in this subsection are included on an audio tape band. So you will need to have your audio tape player close to your computer so that you can switch the tape on and off as necessary.

Nearly all the data sets that you will be exploring and analysing in this chapter (and in the rest of Block D) are large, and simply typing the data into OUStats would occupy a lot of your time. In consequence, all the data sets are provided for you as data files. You will not be asked to enter data sets yourself, either in this block or in assignments, so you will not find any instructions here for entering or editing data. However, instructions have See Appendix 1. been included in an appendix in case you wish to be able to use OUStats to analyse your own data (or in case you are simply interested to know how this is done). Whether or not you study the appendix is entirely up to you.

Like Mathcad, OUStats is a *Windows*-based package, so you should find that your experience with Mathcad will help you as you learn to use OUStats. After you have listened to the audio tape, you will be asked to write down any similarities and differences that you have observed between OUStats and other *Windows*-based packages that you have used (such as Mathcad); so look out for links or distinctions as you work through the tape.

Start up OUStats now, as follows.

◇   *Windows 3.1*: Double-click on the **OUStats** icon in the **MST121 Block D** window.

◇   *Windows 95*: Click on the **Start** menu, move the mouse pointer to **Programs**, then to **MST121 Block D** and click on **OUStats**.

Click again with the mouse, and you should see the opening screen shown in Figure 3.1.

![OUStats window screenshot]

```
OUStats for MST121 - UNTITLED                                    _ 🗗 ✕
File  Edit  Stats  Plot  Options  Window  Help
 UNTITLED                                                       _ ⬜ ✕
        V1          V2          V3          V4          V5        V6
  1
  2
  3
  4
  5
  6
  7
  8
  9
 10
 11
 12
 13
 14
 15
```

Figure 3.1   The opening screen in OUStats

By the way, you can exit from OUStats at any time, simply by clicking on **File** and choosing **Exit** (by clicking on it).

If possible, work through the audio band without a break. But should you have to interrupt your study, you may not need to go back to the beginning of the audio tape and start again. There is one place, about halfway through the tape, from which you could continue; this is indicated clearly in the commentary.

Now listen to Audio Tape 4, Band 1, 'Introducing OUStats for MST121'.

Activity 3.1   *Similarities and differences*

Before reading on, pause for a few minutes to make a note of any similarities and differences you found between OUStats and Mathcad. Some operations are carried out in a similar way using similar menus. It is useful to recognise what these are: these are operations which you could carry out simply from your knowledge of Mathcad.

Comment

Both Mathcad and OUStats are *Windows*-based software packages. Several of the menus look similar and do similar things: **File**, **Edit**, **Window** and **Help**. Both packages have a status bar. In OUStats, at different times the status bar shows either what has just been done or else offers hints on what to do next; whereas in Mathcad, although it sometimes shows hints on what to do, this bar is used more to show the status – that is, auto/manual calculate or wait.

Differences between the packages include the following. In Mathcad, data calculations and plots can appear in one window, whereas OUStats has separate windows for data, output from calculations, and plots. In OUStats, a statistical analysis is carried out simply by clicking on a menu command and completing a dialogue, whereas in Mathcad you would have to enter the appropriate expressions or create graphs in your document.

For reference purposes, below is a brief summary of the main facilities of OUStats that were introduced on the audio tape.

(1) The menus

The **File** and **Edit** menus contain commands for handling and editing files.

The **Stats** menu contains commands for calculations.

The **Plot** menu contains commands for obtaining diagrams.

The **Options** menu allows you to change some of the settings of OUStats – the size of the text in output and the number of significant figures shown in displayed data. You can also access the Calculator resident in *Windows* via this menu.

The **Window** menu contains commands for arranging windows on the screen. (These are standard *Windows* operations.)

The **Help** menu provides access to on-line help.

(2) Data files

To open a data file:

◇ click on **File** and choose **Open**... (by clicking on it) – a dialogue box appears;

◇ click on the file name (the file names are listed on the left of the dialogue box), then click OK.

Information about the data in the file currently open can be obtained by choosing **Notes** in the **File** menu.

(3) Summary statistics

To obtain summary statistics for a variable in an open data file:

◇ click on **Stats**, then choose **Summary statistics**... (by clicking on it);

◇ select the variable name in the dialogue box which appears (by clicking on it), then click OK.

The summary statistics are displayed in the *Output* window.

(4) Frequency diagrams

To obtain a frequency diagram:

◇ click on **Plot**, then choose **Frequency diagram**... (by clicking on it);

◇ select the variable name in the dialogue box which appears (by clicking on it);

◇ enter values in the boxes labelled **First interval starts at** and **Width of intervals** (should you not want the software to choose these values automatically), then click OK. (Note that, in order to override the values chosen automatically, you must replace AUTO by a number in **Width of intervals**.)

Each diagram produced is displayed in a separate *Plot* window (labelled 'Frequency diagram' in this case).

(5) Fitting a normal curve to data

To fit a normal curve:

◇   obtain a frequency diagram for the data;

◇   change this into a histogram with total area 1 by clicking the *right* mouse button and choosing **Histogram**;

◇   click on the *right* mouse button again, and choose **Fit normal curve**;

◇   enter the mean and standard deviation of the required normal curve in the dialogue box, then click OK. (The default values are the sample mean and sample standard deviation.)

The normal curve with the specified mean and standard deviation is then superimposed on the histogram.

(6) Finding areas under a normal curve

To find an area under a normal curve, you must first:

◇   click on **Stats**, then choose **Normal tables**... (by clicking on it);

◇   enter the mean and standard deviation of the required normal distribution in the dialogue box that appears, and click OK.

A screen similar to that in Figure 3.2 will appear.

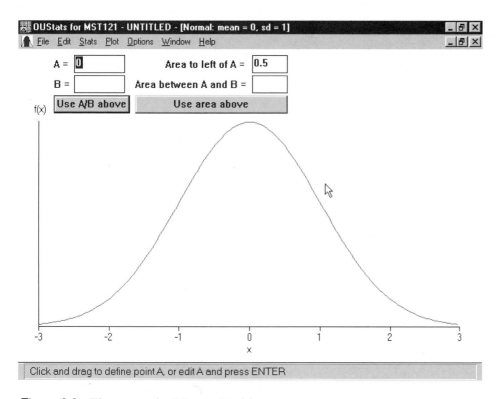

Figure 3.2   The screen for **Normal tables**...

To find the area to the left of a numerical value, z (say):

◇   either position the mouse pointer close to the horizontal axis, hold the mouse button down and drag the mouse until the value in the **A** box is as close as possible to z, then let go of the mouse button;

◇   or edit the value in the **A** box to read z and click on the **Use A/B above** button.

The area to the left of z will appear in the **Area to left of A** box.

You may position the mouse pointer anywhere in the window, but you will probably find it more useful to position it close to the horizontal axis.

To find the area between two values a and b:

◇   enter the value a in the **A** box by either of the methods just described;

◇   enter the value b in the **B** box by either of the methods just described.

If you choose to press and drag the mouse, then the area under the curve between a and b is shaded as soon as you let go of the mouse button, and the area is given in the **Area between A and B** box. If you edit the values, then the area is shaded and its value is given as soon as you click on the **Use A/B above** button.

To find the value z such that the area to the left of z is equal to a numerical value p (say):

◇   double-click in the **Area to left of A** box and type in the number p;

◇   click on the **Use area above** button.

The value z will be displayed in the **A** box.

(7) Saving and closing windows

To save a window:

◇   activate the window (by clicking on it if it is visible, or by choosing its name via the **Window** menu);

◇   click on **File** and choose **Save as**...;

◇   type in the file name and click OK.

The recommended file name extensions are as follows.

Type of window	Extension
Data	.OUS
Notes	.TXT
Output	.LIS
Plot	.WMF

The computer operating system does not distinguish between upper- and lower-case letters in file names: you can use either. For clarity of presentation, we have used upper-case letters in file names in this computer book.

If you save the output window or a plot window, then you may be able to insert these files into a word-processor document. (You will need to consult the documentation accompanying your word-processing package to find out whether it can handle such files and, if so, how to insert them into a document.) Note that .LIS and .WMF files cannot be reopened within OUStats.

If you make any changes to one of the data files supplied with OUStats, and you wish to save the amended data window, then you must do so using **Save as**... from the **File** menu, and you must save it using a different name: all the data files and notes files supplied are protected so that you cannot accidentally change the contents of the original files.

To close a window:

◇   activate the window;

◇   click on **File** and choose **Close**.

When a data file is opened, any previously-saved files are closed down automatically. You will receive a prompt inviting you to save the data window if it has been changed, and the output window if it has been used.

You will not be asked if you wish to save a plot window; the contents of any plot windows that have not been saved previously are lost when you open another data file. If you want to save a plot window, then you must save it before opening another data file.

(8) Using frequency data

Some data are stored in two columns in a data file, with values in one column and corresponding frequencies in the next. When using such data – to obtain summary statistics or a frequency diagram, for instance – the two column names appear on a single line in the dialogue box, with a vertical bar between them: for example, Value | Frequency.

(9) General notes on using OUStats

◇ The status bar at the bottom of the OUStats screen provides hints on what to do next. You will find it helpful to develop a habit of referring to the status bar as you work with OUStats.

◇ When looking at menus and dialogue boxes, you may have noticed that some items are bold while others are faint. An item can be chosen only when it is shown in bold. If an item is faint, then something else must be done before it can be chosen (for example, opening a file, selecting a variable, etc.).

A comment on frequency diagrams

Before you move on to the next group of computer activities in Subsection 3.2, there is one point concerning frequency diagrams that ought to be mentioned. When using a computer package, it is all too easy to obtain a frequency diagram without giving much thought to whether the diagram you obtain is the 'best' possible. Different choices of starting values and interval widths will, in general, produce different diagrams representing the same data; and not all choices of the starting value and interval width will necessarily be appropriate for the data.

Consider, for instance, the two frequency diagrams for the heights of 1000 Cambridge men produced in the audio tape session. The first was obtained by allowing OUStats to select automatically the starting value of the first interval and the width of the intervals. For the second, we chose these values ourselves: since the heights ranged from 62 to 77, it seemed reasonable to choose 60 as the starting value and 2 as the interval width. But were these good choices?

You may recall that the heights were recorded to the nearest inch. (This information is given in **Notes** and was mentioned when the data were introduced in Section 1.) This means that, for instance, the heights of men who were anywhere between 61.5 and 62.5 inches tall were recorded as 62 inches, the heights of men between 62.5 and 63.5 inches tall were recorded as 63 inches, the heights of men between 63.5 and 64.5 inches tall were recorded as 64 inches, and so on.

For the second frequency diagram, we specified that the first interval should start at 60 and have width 2. So OUStats included in this interval all heights recorded as at least 60 inches but less than 62 inches; there were none, since the lowest recorded height was 62 inches. The second interval included all heights recorded as at least 62 inches but less than 64 inches, that is, all those recorded as either 62 inches or 63 inches; there were 23 of these. So there were 23 men between 61.5 and 63.5 inches tall. The heights of these men were represented on the frequency diagram by a bar drawn from 62 to 64, when clearly a bar drawn from 61.5 to 63.5 would have been better.

This sort of discrepancy can be avoided by noting how the data were recorded and choosing intervals appropriately. In this case, since the shortest recorded height was 62 inches and heights between 61.5 and 62.5 inches were recorded as 62, it would be sensible to choose 61.5 as the starting value of the first interval, rather than 60 or 62. Then the first bar would be drawn from 61.5 to 63.5. By the way, the frequency diagram in Figure 1.2 of Chapter D2 can be obtained by using a starting value of 61.5 for the first interval and an interval width of 1.

The important message to be obtained from this example is that when you use a statistics software package, you need to think about what you are doing. Although a package will save you all the work involved in doing calculations and drawing diagrams, it will not think for you. It will usually do whatever you ask it to, whether or not your instructions are sensible or appropriate.

3.2 Is a normal model a good fit?

In Subsection 3.1, a normal curve was chosen to model the variation in the heights of Cambridge men, but no check was made on whether the model was a 'good' fit. In this subsection, we shall use OUStats to investigate informally for several samples of data whether a fitted normal curve is a good model for the variation observed in the data.

The first stage in investigating whether a normal distribution is a suitable model should always be to obtain a frequency diagram for the data, and to inspect its shape. If it is clearly not bell-shaped – for example, if it is skewed or has more than one clear peak, such as for the four frequency diagrams in Figure 1.4 of Chapter D2 – then a normal model can be rejected immediately. But if it looks as though a bell-shaped curve might be a suitable model for the variation in the data (as in Figure 1.5), then the next step is to fit a normal curve with parameters μ, estimated by the sample mean $\overline{x}$, and σ, estimated by the sample standard deviation s. The fit of the curve can then be inspected by eye.

Sometimes (as was the case for the heights of Cambridge men) a histogram for the data and the fitted normal curve are so similar in shape that it is clear that the model is a good one. But more commonly, perhaps because of the jaggedness of the histogram, there is some doubt about the fit. The problem is to decide whether the differences between the histogram and the curve could be the result of chance, and just a feature of the particular sample, or whether they are an indication that the model is not a good fit.

There are formal statistical tests that can be carried out, called goodness-of-fit tests, for deciding whether a chosen model is a good one for the variation in a sample of data; and if you study statistics in the future, then you will almost certainly meet such tests. However, in this course, we shall adopt a more informal approach: we shall use simulations to generate samples from the chosen normal distribution. This will give us an indication of the nature of the variation that occurs by chance, and thus offer a yardstick against which to judge whether the data could reasonably be thought to be a sample from the chosen normal distribution.

In the following activities, you are invited to explore whether a normal model is a good fit for each of a number of data sets. In the first activity, you are asked to decide for each data set, by looking at a frequency diagram, whether a normal curve is even worth considering. In each of the subsequent activities, you are asked to fit a normal model, and then use simulations to investigate the suitability of the model.

Activity 3.2   Is a normal model worth considering?

In this activity, for each data set, you should obtain a frequency diagram for the data and hence decide whether or not a normal distribution might be suitable for modelling the observed variation. For each data set, you should go through the following steps:

◇   open the data file;

◇   read the information about the data contained in **Notes**;

◇   obtain a frequency diagram for the data, taking particular care over your choice of the interval width and the starting value for the first interval;

◇   decide whether or not you think a normal distribution might be suitable for modelling the observed variation, explaining your decision briefly.

Instructions are given for the first data set only.

(a) The file DIPPER.OUS contains the weights in grams of 198 Irish dipper nestlings at age 6–8 days. Open the data file now. (Choose **Open**... from the **File** menu, and click on DIPPER.OUS, and then OK.) Read the information on these data contained in **Notes**. (Choose **Notes** from the **File** menu.)

You will need to scroll through the list of file names to find the file.

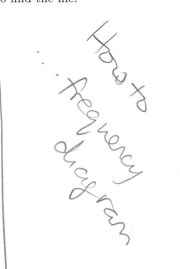

The weights are grouped – the individual weights are not given. The groups are listed in the first column of the data window, the mid-points of the groups are in the second column (labelled 'Weight') and the frequencies in the third column. To represent these data sensibly on a frequency diagram, you need to start the first interval at 9 and use 2 as the interval width.

Obtain a frequency diagram for the data using these values. (Choose **Frequency diagram**... from the **Plot** menu, click on Weight | Frequency, enter 9 and 2 as the starting value for the first interval and the interval width, respectively, and finally click on OK.)

Now consider whether a normal distribution might be suitable for modelling the variation in the data. Questions you might consider include the following. Is the frequency diagram roughly bell-shaped, or is it skewed? Does it have more than one peak?

(b) Repeat the process in part (a) for the data on radial velocities of stars which are contained in the data file RADIAL.OUS.

(c) Repeat the process in part (a) for the data on the lengths of sentences written by H. G. Wells which are contained in the data file AUTHORS.OUS.

(d) Repeat the process in part (a) for the data on the lengths of cuckoo eggs which are contained in the data file CUCKOOS.OUS.

Comment

A solution is given on page 78.

In each of the next three activities, you should:

◇ fit a normal curve to the data;

◇ generate random samples from the fitted normal distribution;

◇ compare frequency diagrams for the random samples with a frequency diagram for the data.

Fairly detailed instructions are given in the first activity below. You should follow a similar procedure for the other two.

Activity 3.3 Weights of Irish dipper nestlings

(a) *Fitting a normal curve*

Open the data file DIPPER.OUS, and obtain a frequency diagram for the data using a first interval value of 9 and an interval width of 2 (as you did in Activity 3.2).

Fitting a normal curve is done in two stages: first, the frequency diagram is rescaled so that its total area is equal to 1; then a normal curve is fitted. These stages are described below.

Click anywhere on the frequency diagram using the *right* mouse button, and choose **Histogram** from the options that appear. The frequency diagram is rescaled.

Now click on the *right* mouse button again, and choose the extra option that appears: **Fit normal curve**. A dialogue box appears.

You must now enter the parameters of the normal curve to be fitted. As we observed in Section 2, the sample mean and sample standard deviation are often used for the parameters of the normal model. The default values given in the dialogue box are the sample mean and sample standard deviation. Their values are displayed to six significant figures – in this case, the values displayed are 27.9394 and 7.74704, respectively – and stored to even greater accuracy.

These statistics are chosen because they are estimates for the population mean and population standard deviation; but it would not be reasonable to suppose or claim six-figure accuracy for these estimates. *As a rough guide, it is reasonable to quote sample statistics to one significant figure more than is given in the data used to calculate them.* The weights of the Irish dipper nestlings are given to two significant figures (roughly), so three-significant-figure accuracy is appropriate for the sample mean and sample standard deviation.

It is a good idea to jot down the parameters of the normal curve you fit, as you will be needing them again later.

Enter the values 27.9 and 7.75 for the mean and standard deviation of the normal curve. Click on OK, and the normal curve is fitted over the histogram.

It looks as though a normal curve fits the data quite well, although the frequency diagram is quite jagged. To see whether this is the sort of jaggedness that might be expected to occur by chance, we shall compare this data set with some random samples *of the same size* drawn from the normal distribution that we have fitted to the data. The sample size is important here: because of the 'settling down' effect, we should expect small samples to produce more jagged frequency diagrams than large ones, so we must compare the frequency diagrams of random samples of the same size as the sample of data.

(b) *Obtaining random samples from the fitted normal distribution*

Random samples from a normal distribution are obtained using **Normal samples**... from the **Stats** menu. Click on **Stats** and choose **Normal samples**... – a dialogue box appears. Enter 27.9 for the mean and 7.75 for the standard deviation: these are the parameters of the normal curve you just fitted. The sample size should be the same as for the data, 198 in this case. To generate 3 samples, set the number of samples to 3. Finally, click OK.

The samples are generated and stored in the first three empty columns in the data window: the columns are labelled Random1, Random2 and Random3.

(c) *Comparing the random samples and the data*

We want to compare the frequency diagram of the data with frequency diagrams for the random samples. We shall use the same intervals for all the samples. Before obtaining the frequency diagrams, we need to decide on the starting value for the first interval; and to do this we need to know the lowest value that appears in any of the samples. This could be found by looking at the data and picking out the lowest value, but this is a tedious exercise for large sample sizes. An alternative is to use **Summary statistics**...: the minimum is one of the statistics displayed.

Choose **Summary statistics**... from the **Stats** menu. You can select several variables at the same time by pressing and dragging: press down the mouse button on Random1, and drag the mouse until Random1, Random2 and Random3 are all highlighted, then release the mouse button. Click OK, and summary statistics for all three samples will be displayed in the output window. Pick out the minimum value for each random sample. (You will need to scroll through the output window to see them.)

The minimum value in one of my samples was 2.13 – this was the lowest of the three minimum values – so I decided to use 1 as the starting value for the first interval for my frequency diagrams (instead of 9, which I used for the data earlier). Your random samples will be different from mine, so you may need to use a different starting value. Do not forget that we want intervals 9–11, 11–13, and so on, so the starting value of the first interval must be an odd number.

Now we have all the information we need. Choose **Frequency diagram**... from the **Plot** menu, and select all of Weight | Frequency, Random1, Random2 and Random3 by pressing and dragging the mouse. Input your starting value for the first interval and 2 for the interval width, then click OK; the four frequency diagrams will be displayed.

(d) *Viewing the frequency diagrams*

You now have five plot windows, the output window and the data window open. Use **Tile** from the **Window** menu so that you can see them all. Close the output window as it is no longer needed (there is no need to save it); and minimise the data window and the window containing the histogram with the fitted normal curve (by clicking on the relevant button in the top right-hand corner of each window – see Figure 3.3). Now use **Tile** again so that you can see the four frequency diagrams together and all the same size. My four diagrams are shown in Figure 3.4.

Windows 3.1   Windows 95

Figure 3.3 Buttons for minimising a window

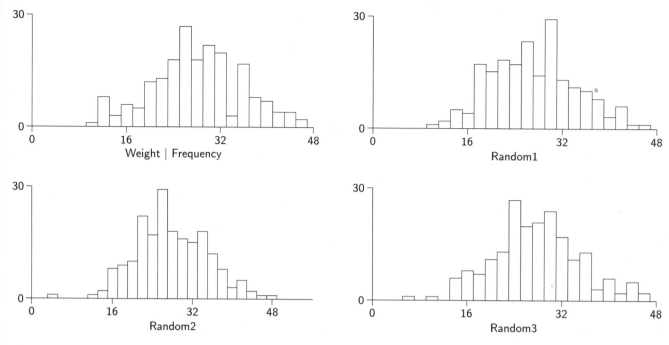

Figure 3.4 Four frequency diagrams from OUStats

We are now in a position to compare the variation in the random samples from the normal distribution that we fitted with that in the data, and hence to decide informally whether or not the model is a good fit. As you can see, the variability evident in the frequency diagrams for the random samples is broadly similar to that in the frequency diagram for the data. So it looks as though the normal distribution is indeed a good model for the variation in the weights of Irish dipper nestlings aged 6–8 days.

Your random samples will be different from mine. Are your frequency diagrams similar in shape to those I obtained? Notice that the scales on all my frequency diagrams are the same. However, this may not have been so for your diagrams: the scales depend on the values in the samples being represented, and three of the samples were random samples. When the scales are different, it is difficult to compare frequency diagrams, so ideally the scales should be adjusted before making a comparison. The box following this activity explains how you can change the size of a window on the screen (and so adjust the scales on the axes).

Changing the size of a window using the mouse

When the mouse pointer is positioned on the border of a window, a double arrow across the border replaces the mouse pointer on the screen. To make a window wider or narrower, place the mouse pointer on either the left or the right edge of the window so that this double arrow is showing. Then press down the mouse button and drag the mouse sideways. When you release the mouse button, the window will be redrawn with the edge in the new position. Similarly, you can make a window taller by pressing and dragging while the mouse pointer is positioned on either the top or the bottom edge of the window. Any diagram inside the window is rescaled to fit the new window.

Activity 3.4   Radial velocities

Repeat the steps described in Activity 3.3 to investigate whether a normal model is a good fit for the variation observed in the radial velocities which are contained in the data file RADIAL.OUS.

Comment

Some comments are given on page 78.

Activity 3.5   Lengths of cuckoo eggs

Repeat the steps described in Activity 3.3 to investigate whether a normal model is a good fit for the variation observed in the lengths of cuckoo eggs which are contained in the data file CUCKOOS.OUS.

Comment

Some comments are given on page 79.

Generating random samples: a summary

Random samples from a normal distribution are obtained using **Normal samples**... from the **Stats** menu using the following steps.

◇   Choose **Normal samples**... from the **Stats** menu.

◇   Enter the mean and standard deviation of the normal distribution, the sample size and the number of samples required in the dialogue box, and click OK.

If k samples are generated, then they are stored in the first k available columns in the data window and are named Random1, Random2, ..., Random$k$.

Note that the number of rows in the data file imposes an upper limit on the size of samples that can be generated. This varies from file to file; you can find the maximum sample size by scrolling down the data window. The number of columns in the data file imposes an upper limit on the number of random samples that can be generated.

Normal samples and random numbers

The command **Normal samples**..., which is contained in the **Stats** menu of OUStats, allows you to generate samples of values chosen randomly from a normal distribution. You may have wondered how this is done.

It may seem paradoxical to use a computer to produce 'random' numbers: we expect any computer program to produce output that is entirely predictable. Nevertheless, computer 'random number generators' are in common use; these generate sequences of 'random' integers. Given an initial value – the *seed* value – the sequence generated is predictable and therefore it is not truly random. Numbers generated in this way are called *pseudo-random* numbers. However, in practice, sequences of pseudo-random numbers are indistinguishable from sequences of random numbers, so they may be regarded as sequences of random numbers and used to simulate random samples in statistical simulations.

Most computer programming languages have a routine that generates pseudo-random integers between zero and the maximum integer N that can be stored by the computer. These integers can be used to generate 'random' values from any distribution – normal, geometric or whatever. Unfortunately, the details of how this is done are beyond the scope of this course.

The MST121 statistics software uses your computer's clock to determine the seed value of the underlying random number generator, thus ensuring that each statistical experiment (using Simulations) or random sample is different. For example, each time you use the **Normal samples**... command in OUStats, the seed value is set using the current date and time, making it extremely unlikely that the samples you obtain are the same as any you have obtained previously.

Note that for lotteries, premium bonds, etc., random simulations based on a pre-programmed algorithm are not used as they could be open to discovery. Instead, some physical randomising device is used. One such device is based on the number of electrons moving inside a valve.

3.3 Printing with OUStats

The main steps involved in printing with OUStats are set out below.

First, make sure that your printer is connected, is installed under *Windows*, and is switched on.

To print a window from OUStats:

◇ activate the window you want to print by clicking on it (or by choosing its title from the **Window** menu);

◇ choose **Print**... from the **File** menu, and click OK.

The contents of the window will then be printed.

You may like to use the following activity to check that you can print output from OUStats.

Activity 3.6   Printing windows from OUStats

Open the file DIPPER.OUS.

Calculate summary statistics for the weights of the Irish dipper nestlings; these are displayed in the output window.

Now obtain a frequency diagram for the data; this is displayed in a plot window.

Now print each of the two windows that have been produced, following the instructions for printing given above.

Before you start the next section, spend a few minutes reflecting on your progress using OUStats. The next activity will help you to do this.

Activity 3.7   Progress with OUStats

How did your experience of using a *Windows*-based software package such as Mathcad help you when you started to use OUStats? Did you get to grips with the basic features of OUStats fairly quickly? Did your experience of using Mathcad give you confidence when tackling a new software package?

Have you found OUStats straightforward to use so far? What did you find easy? Is there any feature of OUStats that you found difficult to understand?

Chapter D2
Section 4   Are people getting taller?

K. Pearson and A. Lee, 'On the laws of inheritance in man', *Biometrika* 2 (1903) pages 357–462.

In the second half of the 19th century, considerable interest developed in the inheritance of characteristics, both in plants and in animals and humans. In the 1890s, Karl Pearson (1857–1936) determined to obtain data on three physical measurements – height, span of arms and length of left forearm – for a large number of families. Many of the data were collected by college students, some of whom made measurements on as many as twenty families. The data were collated by Dr Alice Lee, a colleague of Pearson's at University College, London; she calculated various statistics and prepared some 78 tables of data. According to Pearson, 'this occupied her spare time for nearly two years'. In 1903, several of these tables were published in an article in the journal *Biometrika*.

The box opposite is a verbatim extract from the instructions given to those who collected the data.

The instruction sheet also contained diagrams illustrating the second and third measurements described. The data cards on which the measurements were recorded emphasised that 'both father and mother are absolutely necessary and should not be over 65 years of age' and that neither parent should be a step-parent. All measurements were recorded to the nearest quarter of an inch, although the heights were rounded to the nearest inch before tabulation. A great deal of thought went into the instructions and the design of the data cards. For example, experiments were carried out into the effect of wearing boots on measured heights, and as a result it was decided to subtract an inch from the recorded height of each boot-wearer. As well as noting the wearing of boots, collectors were also asked to put L, A or C against all the measurements if a person being measured had ever broken a leg, arm or collar-bone.

All those measured were between 18 and 65 years old. Pearson explained his choice of this restriction on age in the article. He observed that full growth may not be reached until age 25 or thereabouts. However, he realised that insisting that all sons and daughters should be over 25 years old might make collecting the data much more problematic, not least because it might be difficult to interest college students in the project as most of them were aged between 19 and 22.

There was also the fact that fewer families with all the sons and daughters over 25 years old had both parents surviving. So, since growth between 18 and 25 is very small, he fixed on 18 years as the lower age limit. He also observed that, because of the phenomenon of shrinkage with age, it would have been better to take a lower maximum age than 65 years for parents, but this too would have limited the number of available families.

Altogether, over a thousand families were measured. The heights of 1078 father–son pairs and 1375 mother–daughter pairs were included in the results.

FAMILY MEASUREMENTS

Professor KARL PEARSON, of University College, London, would esteem it a great favour if any persons in a position to do so, would assist him by making one set (or if possible several sets) of anthropometric measurements on their own family, or on families with whom they are acquainted. The measurements are to be made use of for testing theories of heredity, no names, except that of the recorder, are required, but the Professor trusts to the *bona fides* of each recorder to send only correct results.

Each family should consist of a father, mother, and at least one son or daughter, not necessarily the eldest. The sons or daughters are to be at least 18 years of age, and measurements are to be made on not more than two sons and two daughters of the same family. If more than two sons or daughters are easily accessible, then not the tallest but the eldest of those accessible should be selected.

To be of real service the whole series ought to contain 1000–2000 families, and therefore the Professor will be only too grateful if anyone will undertake several families for him.

The measurements required in the case of each individual are to be to the nearest quarter of an inch, and to consist of the following.

(I.) *Height.* – This measurement should be taken, if possible, with the person in stockings, if she or he is in boots it should be noted. The height is most easily measured by pressing a book with its pages in a *vertical plane* on the top of the head while the individual stands against a wall.

(II.) *Span of Arms* – Greatest possible distance between the tip of one middle finger and the tip of the other middle finger, the individual standing upright against a wall with the feet well apart and the arms outstretched, – if possible with one finger against a doorpost or corner of the room.

(III.) *The Length of LEFT Forearm* – The arm being bent *as much as possible* is laid upon a table, with the hand flattened and pressed firmly against the table, a box, book, or other hard object is placed on its edge so as to touch the bony projection of the elbow, another so as to touch the tip of the middle finger. Care must be taken that the books are both perpendicular to the edge of the table. The distance between the books is measured with a tape.

Or,
The arm being bent *as much as possible* the elbow is pressed against the corner of a room or the doorpost, the hand being flattened and pressed against the wall. The greatest distance from the tip of the middle finger to the corner or doorpost is to be measured.

In this section, you will have the opportunity to explore the data that Pearson obtained on the heights of father–son pairs. One question we shall investigate is: 'Were the sons taller, on average, than the fathers?' That is, was the phenomenon of increasing stature, which has been observed more recently, evident in these families at the turn of the century? Another question is: 'Did tall fathers tend to have tall sons, and short fathers have short sons?' In this section, you will be able to investigate both these questions using the statistics software. We shall return to the second question in Chapter D5.

Activity 4.1   The data

Click on **Open**... in the **File** menu. The data on father–son heights are contained in the file PEARSON.OUS. Open this data file now.

As you can see, the data are arranged in a frequency table, with the columns containing father's height in inches, son's height in inches and frequency, respectively. You will see that, for example, there was one father–son pair with the father's height recorded as 59 inches and the son's height as 64 inches; and, if you scroll down to row 23, you will see that there were four father–son pairs with the father's height 63 inches and the son's height 67 inches.

For paired data such as these, it is a good idea to begin by obtaining a scatterplot of the data. Click on **Plot** and choose **Scatterplot**...
(by clicking on it). A dialogue box will appear. To obtain a scatterplot with father's height on the x-axis and son's height on the y-axis, select SonHt | Frequency for the Y variable and FatherHt | Frequency for the X variable. Then click OK, and the scatterplot will be displayed in a plot window.

Is there any pattern discernible in the scatterplot? What does this tell you about the heights of the fathers and the sons?

Comment

The scatterplot is shown in Figure 4.1. (After choosing **Scatterplot**...,
I chose **Tile** from the **Window** menu. The data window and the plot window were then displayed side-by-side on the screen. I then adjusted the size of the plot window until the scales on the scatterplot were as shown in Figure 4.1.)

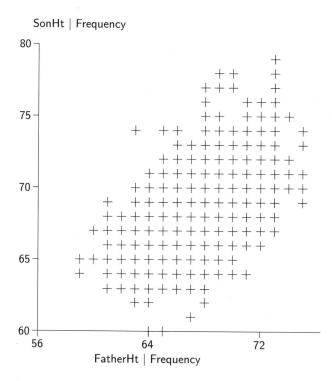

Figure 4.1   A scatterplot of son's height against father's height

Notice that some information is not shown in this scatterplot: it does not show how many father–son pairs there were for each pair of heights, only whether or not there were any pairs. From the scatterplot, it appears that there is a tendency for the taller fathers to have sons taller than those of the shorter fathers. However, there is a lot of scatter, so the relationship between son's height and father's height is a weak one. It is not possible to tell from the scatterplot whether or not the average height of the sons is greater than the average height of the fathers.

Activity 4.2   Average heights

Use **Summary statistics**... to find the mean and standard deviation of the fathers' heights and of the sons' heights. (Select the variables FatherHt | Frequency and SonHt | Frequency to summarise the fathers' heights and sons' heights, respectively.)

Is the average height of the sons greater than the average height of the fathers? Are the sons' heights and the fathers' heights equally variable?

Comment

The sons were taller on average than the fathers – the mean height of the sons was 68.7 inches compared with 67.7 inches for the fathers. The heights of the fathers and the sons were equally variable – the standard deviations (2.75 inches for the sons and 2.72 inches for the fathers) are approximately equal.

Activity 4.3   Modelling the heights

(a) A frequency diagram of the sons' heights is shown in Figure 4.2(a). A normal curve with mean 68.7 and standard deviation 2.75 has been superimposed in Figure 4.2(b).

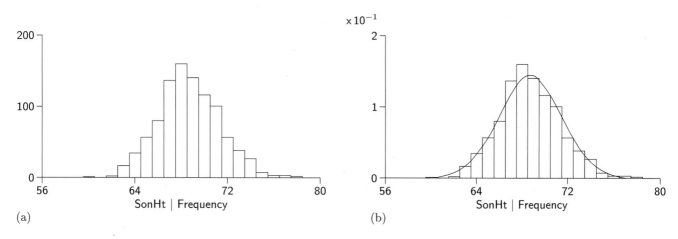

(a)

(b)

Figure 4.2   (a) A frequency diagram   (b) The fitted normal curve

It looks as though a normal distribution models the variation in heights quite well.

Now follow the instructions below for using **Normal tables**... to find the proportion of sons in that generation who were, according to this model, over six feet tall. This proportion is given by the area under the normal curve to the right of 72; this is shown in Figure 4.3.

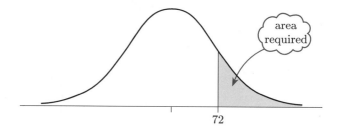

Figure 4.3 The area required

Select **Normal tables**... from the **Stats** menu, and enter 68.7 and 2.75 for the mean and standard deviation, respectively. Click OK, and the normal curve will be displayed.

First, find the area to the left of 72 as follows. Enter 72 in the **A** box and click on the **Use A/B above** button (or press Enter). The area is displayed in the **Area to left of A** box: it is 0.885. Since the total area under any normal curve is 1, the area required is equal to

$$1 - 0.885 = 0.115.$$

So, according to the model, approximately 11.5% of sons of this generation were over six feet tall.

(b) Now fit a normal distribution with mean 67.7 and standard deviation 2.72 to the data on the heights of the fathers. Use this model to estimate the proportion of fathers of this generation who were over six feet tall. Was there a greater proportion of sons over six feet tall than of fathers?

Comment

According to the model for fathers' heights, approximately 5.7% of fathers were over six feet tall. So a greater proportion of sons than fathers were over six feet tall.

In Activity 4.2, you found that the sons were taller, on average, than the fathers. And if anyone whose height is over six feet is regarded as tall, then it appears that there were more 'tall' sons than 'tall' fathers. However, to tackle the question of whether sons are taller than their fathers, we really need to look at the heights of sons whose fathers are of particular heights. For example, is the average height of the sons of fathers who were 64 inches tall greater than 64 inches? And is the average height of the sons of six-foot-tall fathers over six feet? You are asked to investigate questions such as these in the next three activities. The data are stored in a convenient form in the file SONS.OUS, so use this file for these activities. (The data in SONS.OUS and PEARSON.OUS are exactly the same; they are just arranged differently.)

Activity 4.4   Modelling sons' heights

In Activity 4.1, it was observed that sons of tall fathers tended to be taller than sons of short fathers. But if we know the height of a father, what precisely can we say about the height of his son? In this activity, you are invited to explore the heights of sons of fathers of various different heights.

(a) The data on the heights of sons of fathers who were 69 inches tall are contained in the columns named SonHt69 and Freq69 in the file SONS.OUS. Obtain a frequency diagram for these data.

You should find that it looks as though a normal distribution might provide a reasonable model for the variation in these heights. So fit a normal model to these data. (Remember to use one significant figure more for the parameters of the normal distribution than are given in the data: in this case, this means estimating the mean height to one decimal place and the standard deviation to two decimal places.)

According to the model, what proportion of the sons of 69-inch-tall fathers were more than 69 inches tall (and so taller than their fathers)?

(b) Investigate the heights of sons of fathers who were 71 inches tall. (The data are in the columns SonHt71 and Freq71.) Fit a normal distribution to the heights, and use it to estimate the proportion of sons of 71-inch-tall fathers who were taller than their fathers.

(c) Investigate the heights of sons of fathers who were 67 inches tall and of sons of fathers who were 64 inches tall. (These data are in the pairs of columns SonHt67, Freq67 and SonHt64, Freq64, respectively.) In each case, use a normal distribution to estimate the proportion of sons who were taller than their fathers.

Investigate the heights of sons for fathers of heights of your own choice. Make a note of your results. (The heights of sons for fathers who were *mn* inches tall are in the pair of columns SonHt*mn* and Freq*mn*, as you might expect.)

Comment

(a) Using a normal distribution with mean 69.5 and standard deviation 2.30, I found that the area to the left of 69 was equal to 0.414. So the proportion of sons over 69 inches tall was, according to the model, $1 - 0.414 = 0.586$, or approximately 59%.

(b) Using a normal distribution with mean 70.4 and standard deviation 2.48, I found that the area to the left of 71 was equal to 0.596. So the proportion of sons over 71 inches tall was, according to the model, $1 - 0.596 = 0.404$, or approximately 40%.

(c) Using a normal distribution with mean 68.0 and standard deviation 2.21, I found that the area to the left of 67 was equal to 0.325. So the proportion of sons over 67 inches tall was, according to the model, $1 - 0.325 = 0.675$, or approximately 68%.

Using a normal distribution with mean 66.6 and standard deviation 2.17, I found that the area to the left of 64 was equal to 0.115. So the proportion of sons over 64 inches tall was, according to the model, $1 - 0.115 = 0.885$, or approximately 89%.

Activity 4.5   Conclusions

Look again at the results you obtained in Activity 4.4. What conclusions can you draw about how a son's height is related to his father's height?

Comment

More than half the sons of the shorter fathers (64, 67 and 69 inches tall) were taller than their fathers, but less than half the sons of 71-inch-tall fathers were taller than their fathers. It looks as though sons of short men were more likely to be taller than their fathers than were the sons of tall men.

Activity 4.6   Average heights of sons

In Activity 4.4, you found that, according to the models, although more than half the sons of fathers 64 inches, 67 inches or 69 inches tall were taller than their fathers, fewer than half the sons of fathers 71 inches tall were taller than their fathers. In this activity and the next, you are asked to investigate how the mean height of sons varies with father's height. Begin by completing Table 4.1 below. For each father's height, find the mean height of their sons. The four heights already in the table are those you found in Activity 4.4 when fitting normal models to sons' heights.

The quickest way to obtain the means is using **Summary statistics**.... Recall that you can select several variables at the same time by dragging the mouse. (Look again at the instructions given in part (c) of Activity 3.3 (page 24) if you are not sure how to do this.)

Table 4.1

Father's height in inches	Mean height of sons in inches
59	
60	
61	
62	
63	
64	66.6
65	
66	
67	68.0
68	
69	69.5
70	
71	70.4
72	
73	
74	
75	

Comment briefly on your results.

Comment

The means are contained in the file MEANS.OUS in the column SonMeanHt. Open this file now and check your answers.

You can see from the data in the columns FatherHt and SonMeanHt that the mean height of sons increases with father's height. However, the sons of short fathers were not, on average, as short as their fathers; and the sons of tall fathers were not, on average, as tall as their fathers.

Activity 4.7   Looking for a relationship

Now obtain a scatterplot with father's height (FatherHt) on the x-axis and mean son's height (SonMeanHt) on the y-axis. What does the scatterplot tell you about the relationship between the heights of fathers and the mean height of their sons?

Comment

The scatterplot is shown in Figure 4.4.

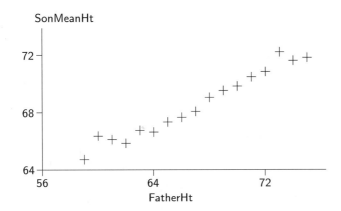

Figure 4.4   A scatterplot of mean son's height against father's height (heights in inches)

From the scatterplot you can see that the mean height of the sons tends to increase with father's height – tall fathers tended to have tall sons, and short fathers tended to have short sons. However, an interesting point emerges from looking more closely at the table of means and the scatterplot – this is that, although tall fathers did tend to have tall sons, on average the height of the sons was less than the height of the fathers; for example, for fathers 73 inches tall, the average height of their sons was approximately 72.2 inches. Similarly, short fathers had sons who were not, on average, as short as themselves.

It was data similar to those collected by Pearson, but on a smaller scale (only about 200 father–son pairs), that led Sir Francis Galton (1822–1911) in the 1880s to the idea of *regression*. Galton called the phenomenon just described 'regression back to the population mean' or, as he put it, 'toward the mediocre'. You can see from the scatterplot that the sample means lie approximately on a straight line, so it would seem reasonable to model the way the mean height of sons depends on father's height by a linear relationship. In Chapter D5, a method is described for choosing a line to model this relationship. The line obtained is called the *least squares fit line* or the *regression line*.

Obtaining a scatterplot: a summary

A scatterplot is obtained using **Scatterplot. . .** from the **Plot** menu using the following steps.

◇   Choose **Scatterplot. . .** from the **Plot** menu.

◇   Select a variable name for the Y variable and a variable name for the X variable, and click OK.

Chapter D2
Section 5   *Exploring normal distributions*

In this section, you are invited to use OUStats to explore the properties of normal distributions. You will need to use **Normal tables...** from the **Stats** menu for all the activities. In general, you will probably find it quicker and easier to edit the values in the boxes than to use the mouse to mark areas under the normal curves.

Activity 5.1   *Different means*

For each pair of values of the parameters μ and σ in the table below, find the area under the normal curve between the values $a = \mu - \sigma$ and $b = \mu + \sigma$.

μ	σ	a $(= \mu - \sigma)$	b $(= \mu + \sigma)$	Area under curve between a and b
0	1	−1	1	
2.5	1	1.5	3.5	
−3	1	−4	−2	

What do you notice?

Comment

A solution is given on page 80.

Activity 5.2   *Different standard deviations*

(a) For each pair of values of the parameters μ and σ in the table below, find the area under the normal curve between the values $a = \mu - \sigma$ and $b = \mu + \sigma$.

μ	σ	a $(= \mu - \sigma)$	b $(= \mu + \sigma)$	Area under curve between a and b
0	1	−1	1	
0	5	−5	5	
0	140	−140	140	

(b) What do you notice? The results obtained in this activity and in Activity 5.1 illustrate a general result for normal distributions. Write down what you think this result might be. Test your conjectured 'result' for a pair of values of μ and σ of your own choice.

Comment

A solution is given on page 80.

Activity 5.3   *Two standard deviations from the mean*

(a) For each pair of values of the parameters μ and σ in the table below, and for a pair of values of your own choice, find the area under the normal curve between the values $a = \mu - 2\sigma$ and $b = \mu + 2\sigma$.

μ	σ	a $(=\mu-2\sigma)$	b $(=\mu+2\sigma)$	Area under curve between a and b
0	1	−2	2	0.976
0	5	−10	10	
20	5	10	30	
20	50			
?	?			

(b) What do you notice? These results illustrate a general result for normal distributions. Write down what you think this result might be. Test your conjectured 'result' for a pair of values of μ and σ of your own choice.

Comment

A solution is given on page 80.

Activity 5.4   *Three standard deviations from the mean*

For each of the pairs of values of μ and σ in the table in Activity 5.3 (including those of your own choice), find the area under the normal curve between $\mu - 3\sigma$ and $\mu + 3\sigma$. Comment on your results.

Comment

A solution is given on page 80.

Activity 5.5   *90% of values*

(a) Consider a normal distribution with parameters $\mu = 0$ and $\sigma = 1$. Follow the instructions below to find the value z such that the area under the normal curve between $-z$ and z is equal to 0.9.

To do this, you must first turn it into a question which you can answer using the **Normal tables**... facility. The software allows you to find a value **A** directly, given the area to the left of **A**, so the first thing to do is to calculate the area to the left of z.

The total area under the normal curve is 1, and the curve is symmetrical about the mean 0; so, if the area between $-z$ and z is 0.9, then the area in each tail (that is, below $-z$ and above z) is equal to $\frac{1}{2} \times 0.1 = 0.05$. This is illustrated in Figure 5.1(a).

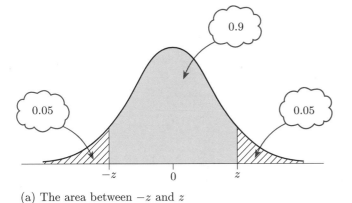

(a) The area between $-z$ and z

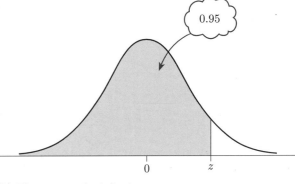

(b) The area to the left of z

Figure 5.1   Finding the area to the left of z

It follows that the total area to the left of z is 0.95; this is shown in Figure 5.1(b). So put 0.95 in the **Area to left of A** box, and click on **Use area above**; the required value z will appear in the **A** box.

(b) Now consider a normal distribution with parameters $\mu = 20$ and $\sigma = 5$. Find the area under the normal curve between the values $\mu - z\sigma$ and $\mu + z\sigma$, where z is the value you found in part (a).

(c) Select values for μ and σ different from those in parts (a) and (b). Find the area under the normal curve between the values $\mu - z\sigma$ and $\mu + z\sigma$, where z is the value you found in part (a).

(d) Suggest a general result for normal distributions.

Comment

A solution is given on page 80.

Activity 5.6   95% of values

(a) Consider a normal distribution with parameters $\mu = 0$ and $\sigma = 1$. Find the value z such that the area under the normal curve between $-z$ and z is equal to 0.95.

(b) Now consider a normal distribution with parameters $\mu = 20$ and $\sigma = 5$. Find the area under the normal curve between the values $\mu - z\sigma$ and $\mu + z\sigma$, where z is the value you found in part (a).

(c) Select values for μ and σ different from those in parts (a) and (b). Find the area under the normal curve between the values $\mu - z\sigma$ and $\mu + z\sigma$, where z is the value you found in part (a).

(d) Suggest a general result for normal distributions.

Comment

A solution is given on page 80.

Activity 5.7   99% of values

(a) Consider a normal distribution with parameters $\mu = 0$ and $\sigma = 1$. Find the value z such that the area under the normal curve between $-z$ and z is equal to 0.99.

(b) Now consider a normal distribution with parameters $\mu = 20$ and $\sigma = 5$. Find the area under the normal curve between the values $\mu - z\sigma$ and $\mu + z\sigma$, where z is the value you found in part (a).

(c) Select values for μ and σ different from those in parts (a) and (b). Find the area under the normal curve between the values $\mu - z\sigma$ and $\mu + z\sigma$, where z is the value you found in part (a).

(d) Suggest a general result for normal distributions.

Comment

A solution is given on page 81.

Chapter D3
Section 3   Confidence intervals on the computer

In Subsection 3.1, you will have the opportunity to use computer simulations to check the interpretation of a 95% confidence interval given in Section 2 of Chapter D3. And in Subsection 3.2, you will learn how to use OUStats to calculate a 95% confidence interval for a population mean from a large sample of data.

3.1   Interpreting a confidence interval

In Section 2, it was stated that if a large number of samples is drawn from a population, and a 95% confidence interval for the population mean is calculated from each sample, then approximately 95% of these confidence intervals will contain the population mean μ. In this subsection, you will have the opportunity to investigate the accuracy of this statement. You will be using the *Simulations* software to generate many samples and to calculate the corresponding confidence intervals.

For each different population distribution that you use, you can investigate what proportion of 95% confidence intervals contain the population mean to ascertain whether it is indeed approximately 95%. The software can be used to simulate taking samples from either a normal distribution or a geometric distribution.

Activity 3.1   Confidence intervals for the mean of a normal distribution

---

(a) Start the *Simulations* software running as follows.

◇   In *Windows 3.1*, double-click with the mouse on the **Simulations** icon in the **MST121 Block D** window.

◇   In *Windows 95*, click on the **Start** menu, move the mouse pointer to **Programs**, then to **MST121 Block D** and click on **Simulations**.

Click again with the mouse to obtain the **Simulations** menu. Now click on **Confidence intervals** to open this simulation.

At the top of the screen are two buttons, labelled **Normal** and **Geometric**. The default option is **Normal**; this is the option you will be using in this activity.

> The **Options** of **Thick lines** and **Tones** are available with this simulation.

(b) The default values of the parameters μ and σ are 0 and 1, respectively; and the default values of the sample size and the number of samples are 25 and 100. Run the simulation with these values to see what happens.

Each confidence interval is represented horizontally on the diagram on the right of the screen. Notice that the population mean μ is marked by a line down the centre of the diagram, and that any confidence interval that does not contain μ is displayed in a different colour from those that do contain μ. Thus it is possible to identify easily those intervals which do not contain μ. When the simulation ends, you can scroll back to see how many of the intervals failed to include the

> There are also dashed lines at distances $\sigma/2$, σ and $3\sigma/2$ from the mean.

population mean. Alternatively, notice that the number of confidence intervals which do contain the population mean μ is displayed in the box in the bottom left-hand corner of the screen.

The first time that I ran the simulation, 94 out of the 100 confidence intervals contained the population mean μ; the other six did not. You may well have obtained a different number. Run the simulation several times, and note down the results. On average, approximately what proportion of your confidence intervals contained the population mean μ?

(c) Run the simulation several times for values of the parameters μ and σ of your own choice, and note down your results.

For each pair of values that you used, on average what proportion of the confidence intervals contained the population mean μ?

(d) Now change the sample size to 100 (say). Run the simulation several times for different values of μ and σ of your own choice, and note down your results in each case.

On average, what proportion of the confidence intervals contained the population mean μ?

(e) Investigate the proportion of confidence intervals which contain the population mean μ for further different sample sizes and parameter values. Note down your results.

(f) Comment briefly on your results and on any points you may have noticed about the confidence intervals you obtained for different sample sizes.

Comment

I ran the simulation ten times for samples of size 25 from a normal distribution with mean 0 and standard deviation 1. I obtained the following results for the number of confidence intervals (out of 100) which contained the population mean μ.

94 92 93 97 94 97 95 97 91 94

That is, 94.4% of all the intervals contained the population mean μ. Another ten simulations produced 93.7% of intervals containing μ. In both cases, the proportion of confidence intervals which contained μ was only a little less than 95%.

For samples of size 100 and $\mu = 50$, $\sigma = 10$, I obtained the following results.

97 94 95 96 94 96 96 97 93 94

Overall, 95.2% of the confidence intervals contained the population mean μ. I used the simulation for various other sample sizes between 40 and 400, and for a number of different parameter values, and in each case obtained similar results: approximately 95% of the confidence intervals contained the population mean μ.

In general, I noticed that (as expected) the confidence intervals were narrower for larger sample sizes. It was observed earlier, in Chapter D2, that the sample standard deviation varies less from sample to sample when the sample size is large than when it is small. So we should expect the width of the confidence intervals to vary less from sample to sample for the larger sample sizes. This was so for my simulations. Did you notice that there was less variation in the width of the confidence intervals for the larger sample sizes that you tried than for the smaller sample sizes?

Activity 3.2   *Confidence intervals for the mean of a geometric distribution*

Now click on the **Geometric** button. The default value of the parameter p is $\frac{1}{2}$.

Use this simulation to investigate the proportion of 95% confidence intervals for the mean of a geometric distribution that actually contain the population mean. Run the simulation for various values of the parameter and for various sample sizes from 25 upwards. (Recall from Chapter D1 that the mean of a geometric distribution with parameter p is $1/p$.)

Comment briefly on your results. In particular, write down any points you may have noticed about the lengths of confidence intervals for different sample sizes, and about the proportion of confidence intervals which contain the population mean for different sample sizes.

Comment

I ran the simulation for a range of sample sizes similar to those which I used in Activity 3.1 when investigating confidence intervals for the mean of a normal distribution. I tried several values for the parameter p: $\frac{1}{6}, \frac{1}{2}, \frac{4}{5}, \ldots$. For each parameter value and for each sample size of 50 or larger that I tried, I found that the proportion of confidence intervals that contained the population mean was approximately 95%. However, when I took samples of size 25, the proportion of confidence intervals that contained the population mean was generally a little lower than 95%. For instance, for $n = 25$ and $p = \frac{1}{2}$, just over 91% of my intervals contained the population mean; and for $n = 25$ and $p = \frac{1}{6}$, only about 90% of my intervals contained the population mean. In all cases the proportion was less than 95%.

You may recall that for large sample sizes, the sampling distribution of the mean may be approximated by a normal distribution, and the approximation improves as the size of the samples increases. A geometric distribution is right-skewed (for any value of the parameter p), and the approximation is not nearly as good for samples of size 25 as it is for larger sample sizes. As a result, rather less than 95% of the confidence intervals actually contain the population mean for samples as small as 25.

You may also have noticed that the width of the confidence intervals varied greatly for samples of size 25. This occurs because for samples of size 25 from a geometric distribution, the sample standard deviation varies greatly from sample to sample. As for the normal distribution, the sample standard deviation, and hence the width of the confidence intervals, varies much less from sample to sample for larger sample sizes.

3.2   Calculating a confidence interval

In order to calculate a 95% confidence interval for a population mean, the values of the sample mean $\overline{x}$ and the sample standard deviation s need to be calculated. For large samples, this can be a tedious exercise using a calculator, so you were spared carrying out these calculations in Section 2; in each example and activity, you were given the values of $\overline{x}$ and s.

In this subsection, you will not be given these summary statistics. Instead, you will be given the data in a file, and invited to use OUStats to calculate confidence intervals. The sample mean and sample standard deviation are calculated automatically when using OUStats to find a confidence interval.

In the first activity, you will be shown how to find a confidence interval for the mean height of Cambridge men in 1902. You will be able to check that the calculations agree with those carried out using a calculator in Section 2. You will need to use OUStats for all the activities in this subsection.

Activity 3.3   Finding a confidence interval

The data on the heights of 1000 Cambridge men are contained in the file HEIGHTS.OUS. Open this file now.

A 95% confidence interval for a population mean is obtained using **Confidence interval...** in the **Stats** menu. Click on **Stats**, and choose **Confidence interval...** (by clicking on it). In the dialogue box which appears, select Height | Frequency as the variable (it is the only one available in this case) and click OK; the confidence interval is then calculated.

The output includes the sample mean, sample standard deviation and sample size (for information), and a statement of the 95% confidence interval for the population mean. In this case, the confidence interval given is (68.71, 69.03). So we can be fairly sure that the mean height of all Cambridge men in 1902 was between 68.71 inches and 69.03 inches.

In Section 2, we obtained (68.7, 69.1) for the 95% confidence interval. The slight discrepancy between these two results is due to rounding error: in Section 2, we used values for the mean and standard deviation which had been rounded to 3 significant figures, whereas OUStats calculates the values of the mean and standard deviation to much greater accuracy and uses these values to calculate a confidence interval.

Activity 3.4   Sample size

The procedure described in Section 2 for calculating a 95% confidence interval for a population mean should be used only when the sample size is at least 25. Any results obtained using the formula given there for a smaller sample would be inaccurate and unreliable. In this activity, you are asked to explore what happens if you try to use OUStats to calculate a confidence interval for a sample of fewer than 25 items of data.

The data file BAR.OUS contains data on the gross hourly earnings (in pence) in 1995 of a sample of 14 female bar staff. Open the file now, and instruct the computer to calculate a 95% confidence interval for the mean gross hourly earnings in 1995 for female bar staff. What output do you obtain?

Comment

You will have found that because the sample size is less than 25, the software produces a message telling you that the sample size must be at least 25. However, most statistics packages are not so friendly: if you ask for an inappropriate procedure to be carried out, it will be done. So it is important for you to know when a procedure should or should not be used.

Activity 3.5   Cuckoo eggs

The lengths in millimetres of the 243 cuckoo eggs which were represented in Figure 1.5(d) of Chapter D2 are contained in the file CUCKOOS.OUS. Use these data to find a 95% confidence interval for the mean length of all cuckoo eggs.

Source: O. H. Latter, 'The egg of *Cuculus canorus*', *Biometrika* 1 (1902) 164–176.

Comment

A solution is given on page 81.

Activity 3.6   Authorship and sentence length

In Activity 2.4, you calculated a 95% confidence interval for the mean sentence length in a book by G. K. Chesterton. The data on sentence lengths are contained in the data file AUTHORS.OUS, together with data on sentence lengths in two other books: *The Work, Wealth and Happiness of Mankind* by H. G. Wells and *An Intelligent Woman's Guide to Socialism* by G. B. Shaw. These data were collected by C. B. Williams in an investigation into sentence length as a criterion of literary style. Williams chose these particular books for his investigation because, in his words, 'all three deal with sociological subjects and none of them are in the "conversational style"'.

Source: C. B. Williams, 'A note on the statistical analysis of sentence-length, as a criterion of literary style', *Biometrika* 31 (1940) 356–361.

Open the file AUTHORS.OUS now, and explore its contents; remember that you can obtain information about the data in the file using **Notes** from the **File** menu.

(a) How does the distribution of sentence lengths vary between authors? In order to help you answer this question, obtain frequency diagrams for each of the authors, and compare them.

> *Hint*: Choose **Frequency diagram**... from the **Plot** menu to obtain the diagrams. Then choose **Tile** from the **Window** menu, so that you can view all three diagrams together. The scales on the three diagrams will be different. Remember that you can adjust the size of a window, and hence the scale on the diagram in it, by dragging the mouse.
> If you are not sure how to do this, then look again at the instructions given just before Activity 3.4 of Chapter D2 (page 27 in this book).

(b) Compare the mean sentence lengths for the three authors. Does there appear to be a difference? Which author seems to write the longest sentences? Which author seems to write the shortest sentences?

(c) Find a 95% confidence interval for the mean sentence length in each book. What do you conclude from your results?

Comment

A solution is given on page 81.

Activity 3.7   Birthweights

The file BIRTHWT.OUS contains the birthweights of 37 male and 34 female babies, all of whom were born two weeks 'early', that is, at the end of a 38-week gestation period. Find 95% confidence intervals for the mean birthweight of baby boys born two weeks early and for the mean birthweight of baby girls born two weeks early. Comment on your results.

Comment

A solution is given on page 82.

Calculating confidence intervals: a summary

A 95% confidence interval for a population mean based on a large (≥ 25) sample from the population is obtained using **Confidence interval...** from the **Stats** menu.

◇   Choose **Confidence interval...** from the **Stats** menu.

◇   Select the appropriate variable name in the dialogue box which appears (to indicate the data to be used), and click OK.

If two or more variable names are selected, then a 95% confidence interval is calculated using each column of data selected.

Chapter D4
Section 2   Exploring the data

In this section, the use of OUStats to produce boxplots is illustrated for the data on city block scores which are given in Table 1.1 of Chapter D4. You will be invited to explore the data further to see whether there is a relationship between the time spent memorising the positions of the objects and the score obtained on the test.

Activity 2.1   Obtaining boxplots

The data on city block scores and on memorisation times are contained in the file MEMORY.OUS. Open the file now, and read the information about the data given in **Notes**.

Boxplots are obtained using the **Plot** menu. Click on **Plot**, and choose **Boxplot...** (by clicking on it). To obtain boxplots for the city block scores of the two groups on the same diagram, select EScore and YScore as follows: click on EScore, then, while holding down the Ctrl key, click on YScore; both EScore and YScore should now be highlighted. Click on OK, and the boxplots will be produced.

You should find that the boxplots look similar to those in Figure 1.4 of Chapter D4, although the scale on the axis may not be the same, and the five key values are not displayed. When a boxplot is on the screen, you can display a list of the five key values by pressing and holding down the mouse button while the pointer is within the box or close to either whisker. Try this now. When you release the mouse button, the numbers will disappear.

Now obtain boxplots for the memorisation times of the two groups (on a single diagram). Check that they look similar to those in the solution to Activity 1.5 of Chapter D4.

In Section 1, we observed that the boxplots for the city block scores suggest that, generally, the young people performed better on the test than the elderly people. However, the boxplots for the memorisation times indicate that the young people spent longer studying the positions of the objects. Does spending longer studying the positions improve performance on the test? If so, then this could explain why the young people performed better on the test.

To investigate whether memorisation time and performance on the test are related, we must look at the city block scores and memorisation times of the individuals who took the test. This information is available in the file MEMORY.OUS. The data in the file are paired. For instance, the first entry in the column headed EScore and the first entry in the column headed ETime relate to one person from the elderly group, and so on.

Instructions for obtaining a scatterplot were given in Chapter D2, Activity 4.1 (page 32 in this book).

Activity 2.2 Is performance related to memorisation time?

Obtain two scatterplots, one for the young people and one for the elderly people. Plot memorisation time on the horizontal axis, and city block score on the vertical axis. (Use **Scatterplot...** from the **Plot** menu.) Is there any evidence of a relationship between memorisation time and city block score for either group? Describe any patterns in the scatterplots.

Comment

You should find that in both scatterplots, there is a tendency for the city block score to decrease as the memorisation time increases. However, there is a lot of scatter in the plots, so the relationships are weak.

Activity 2.3 Combining the data

It is difficult to tell from the two separate scatterplots whether a young person and an elderly person who spend similar times studying the positions of the objects obtain similar city block scores. We can investigate this by plotting all the data on the same diagram. Obtain a scatterplot for all 27 people who took the test, with memorisation time on the horizontal axis and city block score on the vertical axis. The data for all 27 people are in the columns headed Score and Time.

What can you deduce from the scatterplot? Is there any evidence that young people do better on the test – that is, have lower city block scores – than elderly people who spend a similar length of time memorising the positions of the objects?

Comment

Figure 2.1 contains a scatterplot showing the city block scores and memorisation times for all 27 people who took the test. Different plotting symbols have been used in this figure for the young and the elderly. (It is not possible to use different symbols using OUStats.)

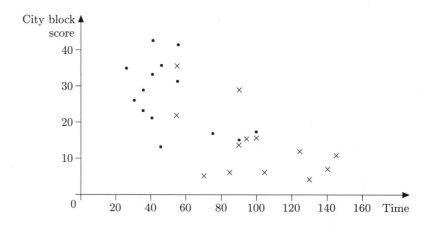

Figure 2.1 A scatterplot of city block scores and memorisation times (× for Young, • for Elderly)

Looking at the scatterplot as a whole, there appears to be a relationship between the time spent studying the positions of the objects and the city block score obtained: in general, the city block score decreases as the memorisation time increases. There is some overlap in the memorisation times of the people in the young and the elderly groups: in each group, there were individuals who spent between 55 and 100 seconds studying the positions of the objects. This part of the scatterplot provides very little evidence that city block scores are lower for young people than for elderly people who spent similar times memorising the positions of the objects.

It seems possible that the better performance of the young group on the test is due to the fact that, in general, they spent longer than the elderly group studying the positions of the objects. Of course, we do not know whether the elderly people would have done as well as the young people if they had all spent the same time studying the positions of the objects.

The final activity in this section will give you some practice at obtaining boxplots on the computer and interpreting them. You will obtain further practice in Section 4.

Activity 2.4   Earnings of primary school teachers

The file PRIMARY.OUS contains data on the gross weekly earnings in 1995 of 91 primary school teachers, of which 54 are women and 37 are men. Obtain boxplots for the earnings of the women and the men. What do the boxplots tell you about the relative earnings in 1995 of male and female primary school teachers?

Comment
A solution is given on page 82.

Obtaining boxplots: a summary

Boxplots are obtained using **Boxplot**... from the **Plot** menu, using the following steps.

◇   Choose **Boxplot**... from the **Plot** menu.

◇   Select one or more variable names (but not more than 10), and click OK.

◇   To display a list of the five key values on a boxplot, press and hold down the mouse button while the pointer is within the box or close to one of the whiskers.

Selecting more than one variable at a time: a summary

In Section 3 of Chapter D2, instructions were given on how to select several adjacent variables at the same time. In this section, you have seen how to select non-adjacent variables together. A summary of these procedures is given below as a reminder and for easy reference.

◇   Variables which are adjacent in a variable list may be selected together by placing the mouse pointer on the first of the variables and dragging the mouse until all the required variables are highlighted. Then release the mouse button.

◇   Variables which are not adjacent in a variable list may be selected together as follows. Click on the first variable required. To select other variables at the same time, hold down the Ctrl key and then click on each of the additional variables required. Then release the Ctrl key.

◇   A variable whose name is already highlighted may be deselected by holding down the Ctrl key and clicking on its name.

In this section, the use of OUStats to carry out a two-sample z-test is explained. An essential first step in any investigation is to look at the data. So, in each case, you will be asked to compare the data visually using boxplots before performing a two-sample z-test.

Activity 4.1   *Wing lengths of meadow pipits*

In this activity, the data from Table 3.1 of Chapter D4 on the wing lengths of male and female meadow pipits will be used to demonstrate the use of OUStats to perform a two-sample z-test.

(a) The data are in the file PIPITS.OUS. Open this file now. Compare the wing lengths of the male and female meadow pipits using boxplots. Check that these boxplots agree with those given in Figure 3.1 of the main text in Chapter D4.

(b) The boxplots suggest that there is a difference between the wing lengths of male and female meadow pipits. So now we shall carry out a two-sample z-test to investigate this apparent difference. The first stage is to write down the null and alternative hypotheses: these are

$$H_0 : \mu_M = \mu_F,$$
$$H_1 : \mu_M \neq \mu_F,$$

where μ_M, μ_F are the mean wing lengths of the populations of male and female meadow pipits, respectively. (These hypotheses were stated in Section 3.)

The second stage is to calculate the test statistic. This is the part of the hypothesis test that the computer can do for you. Click on **Stats**, and choose **Two sample z-test**... (by clicking on it). You need to specify the data to be used. Select MLength (which contains the wing lengths of the males) as the first variable, and FLength (which contains the wing lengths of the females) as the second variable. Click on OK, and the calculations will be performed.

The output includes the mean, the standard deviation and the sample size of each of the two samples, and the test statistic. According to OUStats, the numerical value of z, the test statistic, is 7.562. Notice that this differs slightly from the value we obtained in Section 3: there we obtained $z = 7.63$. This discrepancy is due to rounding error: in Section 3, to calculate the test statistic, we used values of the means and standard deviations which had been rounded to three significant figures, whereas OUStats calculates the means and standard deviations to many more significant figures than this, and then uses these values to calculate the test statistic.

The third and final stage in a hypothesis test is to draw a conclusion (as in Section 3). Since the test statistic z equals 7.562, which is greater than 1.96, we reject the null hypothesis at the 5% significance level in favour of the alternative hypothesis. We conclude that the mean wing length of male meadow pipits is not equal to the mean wing length of female meadow pipits. And since the sample mean is greater for the males than for the females, this suggests that the mean wing length of males is greater than the mean wing length of females.

Activity 4.2   Sample sizes

In Section 1, the city block scores on a memory test of a group of 13 young people and 14 elderly people were compared using boxplots. And, in Section 2, you reproduced these boxplots using OUStats. Since the two-sample z-test depends on the Central Limit Theorem, both sample sizes must be at least 25 for the test to be used. Try using the software to perform the test for the data on city block scores. (The data are in the file MEMORY.OUS.) What happens?

Comment

You will have found that, for these data, the software produces a message telling you the sample sizes and reminding you that both sample sizes must be at least 25. The test is not carried out. This happens whenever either of the sample sizes is less than 25. This is another friendly feature of the software: most statistics packages will carry out your instructions to perform a two-sample z-test whether or not it is an appropriate procedure to use. If it is not appropriate, because the sample sizes are too small, then the results produced using the test would be unreliable and possibly misleading.

Activity 4.3   Authorship and sentence length

In Activity 3.6 of Chapter D3 (page 45 in this book), you explored the distribution of sentence lengths for three books, one by each of three authors – G. K. Chesterton, H. G. Wells and G. B. Shaw. You also obtained confidence intervals for the mean sentence lengths of the three books, and compared them. In this chapter, two methods for comparing samples of data have been described: first boxplots for a visual comparison, and then the two-sample z-test to test for a difference between two population means.

(a) Compare the sentence lengths of the three authors using boxplots (the data are in the file AUTHORS.OUS).

(b) Use the two-sample z-test to investigate whether there is a difference between the mean sentence lengths in the book by G. K. Chesterton and the book by H. G. Wells. State your hypotheses, the test statistic and your conclusion clearly. Note that you should include a statement of your hypotheses, the test statistic and your conclusions in your record of every hypothesis test that you carry out. This applies whether you use a calculator or a computer to carry out the calculations.

(c) Test for a difference between the mean sentence lengths in the book by G. K. Chesterton and the book by G. B. Shaw. Again, state clearly your hypotheses, the test statistic and your conclusion.

Comment

A solution is given on page 83.

Activity 4.4   Birthweights of babies

The file BIRTHWT.OUS contains the birthweights of 37 male and 34 female babies, all of whom were born two weeks 'early', that is, at the end of a 38-week gestation period. In Activity 3.7 of Chapter D3 (page 45 in this book), you found 95% confidence intervals for the mean birthweight of baby boys born two weeks early and for the mean birthweight of baby girls born two weeks early.

(a) Obtain boxplots for the birthweights of the boys and girls. Comment on what they tell you about the birthweights of boys and girls born two weeks early.

(b) Use the two-sample z-test to investigate whether there is a difference between the mean birthweight of boys born two weeks early and the mean birthweight of girls born two weeks early. State clearly your hypotheses, the test statistic and your conclusion.

Comment

A solution is given on page 83.

Activity 4.5   Earnings of primary school teachers

The file PRIMARY.OUS contains data on the gross weekly earnings in 1995 of 91 primary school teachers, of which 54 are women and 37 are men. In Activity 2.4 (page 49 in this book), you compared the earnings of the men and women using boxplots. Use the two-sample z-test to investigate whether there was a difference between the mean gross weekly earnings (in 1995) of male primary school teachers and female primary school teachers. State your hypotheses, the test statistic and your conclusion clearly.

Comment

A solution is given on page 84.

Two-sample z-test: a summary

The two-sample z-test is carried out using **Two sample z-test**... from the **Stats** menu, using the following steps.

◇   Choose **Two sample z-test**... from the **Stats** menu.

◇   Select two variables, one as Variable 1 and one as Variable 2, and click OK.

The test is carried out only if both sample sizes are at least 25. If either sample size is less than 25, then an error message is produced.

Chapter D5
Section 2   *Fitting a line to data*

In this section, OUStats will be used to calculate the least squares fit line for the concrete data given in Section 1. You will then have the opportunity to investigate the relationships between several other pairs of variables. In each case, you will be asked to obtain a scatterplot and, if it seems appropriate, fit a straight line to the data and use the equation of this line to make predictions.

Activity 2.1   *Finding the least squares fit line*

The data on the pulse velocity and crushing strength of concrete given in Table 1.1 of Chapter D5 are contained in the file CONCRETE.OUS.

(a) Open the file now, and obtain a scatterplot of the data with crushing strength along the y-axis and pulse velocity along the x-axis.

   You can display the regression line on the scatterplot as follows.

   Click the *right* mouse button anywhere on the scatterplot; you should see a list of options displayed on the screen. If you select the final option, **Regression line**, then the regression line is added to the scatterplot. Select **Regression line** now by clicking on it.

   The regression line may be removed from the scatterplot by repeating the above steps: click on the scatterplot using the *right* mouse button to obtain the list of options, then 'switch off' the regression line by clicking once more on **Regression line**.

   Click on the right mouse button now, and look at the other options available. The first four options allow you to change the plotting symbol: the default is **Plus**. You can select a different symbol by clicking on it. If the fifth option is selected, the points are joined in the order in which they are listed in the data file. Investigate these options now.

(b) The equation of the least squares fit line is obtained using the **Stats** menu. Choose **Regression...** (by clicking on it). Now select Strength as the Y variable and Velocity as the X variable, and click OK. The equation of the least squares fit line is displayed in the output window in the following form.

```
Regression line
X variable:    Velocity
Y variable:    Strength
n = 14

The equation of the regression line of y on x is

     y = -87.83 + 25.89x
```

So the equation of the least squares fit line is $y = -87.83 + 25.89x$, where y is the crushing strength of concrete and x is the pulse velocity for the concrete. This is the equation that was quoted in Section 1.

Activity 2.2   How tall will my son be?

Pearson's data on the heights of 1078 father–son pairs are contained in the file PEARSON.OUS.

(a) Obtain a scatterplot of son's height against father's height (with father's height along the x-axis), and then add the least squares fit line to the plot.

(b) Obtain the equation of the least squares fit line, and use it to predict the height of the son of a 70-inch-tall man.

(c) By referring to the scatterplot you obtained in part (a), comment on how precise you think this estimate might be.

Comment

A solution is given on page 84.

When will Old Faithful erupt?

See Chapter D2, Activity 1.2.

Every year, tourists flock to the Yellowstone National Park in Wyoming in the United States. One of the attractions is the Old Faithful geyser, which erupts about 20 times a day, on average. As you saw in Chapter D2, the eruptions vary in length, the shortest lasting just over a minute and the longest about 5 minutes. The intervals between eruptions also vary a lot. Sometimes the waiting time from the end of one eruption to the beginning of the next is as short as 40 minutes, but it can be as long as an hour and a half. Unlucky visitors can have a long wait! So is there a way of predicting when the next eruption will occur, so that visitors can be informed?

In August 1978, the geyser was observed between 6 am and midnight on eight consecutive days; the duration of each eruption and the waiting time until the next eruption were both recorded. The purpose of collecting the data was to investigate whether the duration of one eruption could be used to predict when the next is likely to occur. The question was: 'Is there a relationship between the duration of an eruption and the waiting time until the next eruption?' And if there is, can we use the data to formulate a rule for predicting when the next eruption is likely to occur?

RED ALERT!
OLD FAITHFUL IS ABOUT
TO ERUPT AGAIN!

Activity 2.3   Exploring the relationship

The data on the eruptions of the Old Faithful geyser in August 1978 are contained in the file FAITHFUL.OUS.

(a) Obtain a scatterplot with the duration of an eruption along the x-axis and the waiting time until the next eruption along the y-axis.

(b) What does the scatterplot tell you about the relationship between the duration of an eruption and the waiting time until the next eruption? Do you think a straight line would be a suitable model for the relationship?

Comment

A solution is given on page 85.

Activity 2.4   *When will Old Faithful erupt?*

(a) Obtain the equation of the least squares fit line, and use it to predict the waiting time until the next eruption following eruptions which last for the following times.

   (i) 1.5 minutes   (ii) 3 minutes   (iii) 4.5 minutes

(b) Add the least squares fit line to your scatterplot. Comment on how accurate you think your predictions are.

Comment

A solution is given on page 85.

In fact, when the data were collected, an error was made in recording one day's results: the eruption times and intervals between eruptions were paired incorrectly. This meant that there were quite a number of anomalous points which did not fit the general pattern that you observed. So it was thought that a useful prediction rule could not be formulated. The error was discovered only several years later.

Memory and age

In Chapter D4, an investigation into spatial memory in the young and elderly was discussed. Two groups of people, one young and one elderly, tackled a memory test in which eighteen everyday objects were placed on a 10 by 10 square grid. After a person had studied the positions of the objects for as long as they wished, the objects were removed. Then they were asked to replace the objects in the same positions. Two pieces of data were noted for each person: the time spent studying the positions of the objects, and a measure of accuracy of recall – the city block score.

The city block score is described in Chapter D4, Activity 1.1.

Activity 2.5   *Does performance improve with time?*

In Section 2 of Chapter D4, you used OUStats to investigate whether performance on the memory test was related to the time spent memorising the positions of the objects. The data are in the file MEMORY.OUS.

(a) For the elderly group, obtain a scatterplot of city block score against memorisation time. Is there any evidence of a relationship between the time spent memorising the positions of the objects and performance on the test? If you think it appropriate, then fit a line to the data (with memorisation time as the explanatory variable).

(b) Now obtain a similar scatterplot for the young group. Comment on the relationship between the time spent memorising the positions of the objects and performance on the test. If you think it appropriate, then fit a line to the data.

(c) Now obtain a scatterplot for the data for the two groups combined, and fit a line to the data. According to this model, what is the predicted score of a person whose time spent memorising the positions of the objects is as follows?

   (i) 1 minute   (ii) 2 minutes   (iii) 3 minutes

   Comment briefly on your results.

Comment

A solution is given on page 85.

Activity 2.6   Comparing the fit lines

(a) Obtain a printout of the scatterplot for the two groups combined (without the least squares fit line on it).

(b) On this scatterplot, draw the two fit lines you found in parts (a) and (b) of Activity 2.5 – one for the elderly group and one for the young group. Comment briefly on what you deduce from this diagram.

Comment

A solution is given on page 86.

Finding the equation of the regression line: a summary

The equation of the least squares fit line, or the regression line of y on x, is obtained using **Regression...** from the **Stats** menu using the following steps.

◇   Choose **Regression...** from the **Stats** menu.

◇   Select a variable name for the Y variable and a variable name for the X variable, and click OK.

Scatterplots: a summary

A scatterplot is obtained using **Scatterplot...** from the **Plot** menu, using the following steps.

◇   Choose **Scatterplot...** from the **Plot** menu.

◇   Select a variable name for the Y variable and a variable name for the X variable, and click OK.

The least squares fit line may be included on a scatterplot using the following steps.

◇   Click with the *right* mouse button anywhere on the scatterplot.

◇   Choose **Regression line** from the list of options that appears (by clicking on it).

The regression line may be removed by repeating the above steps.

The plotting symbol on a scatterplot may be changed using the following steps.

◇   Click with the *right* mouse button anywhere on the scatterplot.

◇   Choose the symbol you require from the list of options that appears (by clicking on it).

Chapter D5
Section 3   *Fitting a curve to data*

In this section, we discuss briefly the problem of fitting a curve to data. We begin by looking at some data on the population of the USA at ten-year intervals from 1790 to 1910.

Activity 3.1   *Transforming the data*

(a) The US population data are contained in the file USPOP.OUS. Open this file now. Obtain a scatterplot with the US population along the *y*-axis and the year along the *x*-axis.

  Notice that the points do not lie even approximately in a straight line, so a straight line is not an appropriate model for the relationship between the US population and the year. The relationship is not a linear one.

(b) The data may be transformed using **Transform...** from the **Edit** menu. Click on **Edit**, then choose **Transform...** (by clicking on it). At this stage, a dialogue box is displayed. At the top of the dialogue box is a box for entering the expression for the required transformation. Below this appears a list of the variables in the file currently open, and a calculator keyboard.

  The simplest way to enter an expression in the box at the top involves using the list of variable names and the calculator keyboard in the dialogue box. Alternatively, you could type in an expression directly, using the computer keyboard (in which case, variable names must be enclosed in double quotes). We use the first method.

  To transform data by taking natural logarithms (that is, logarithms to the base *e*), choose LN from the calculator keyboard. Do this now by clicking on it (it lies in the top row of the keyboard). LN will appear in the **Expression to calculate** box. Select the name of the variable that you want to transform – in this case, select Population – and click on the **Enter selected variable** button. The variable name is entered in the **Expression to calculate** box enclosed in double quotes. The expression will read LN "Population". Finally, click OK and the transformed data are entered in the first available empty column, which is renamed automatically. In this case, it is renamed LNPopulation.

(c) Obtain a log–lin plot of the data, as follows. Obtain a scatterplot with LNPopulation along the *y*-axis and Year along the *x*-axis.

  Do you think it would be appropriate to fit a straight line to this scatterplot?

Comment

The log–lin plot I obtained is shown in Figure 3.1.

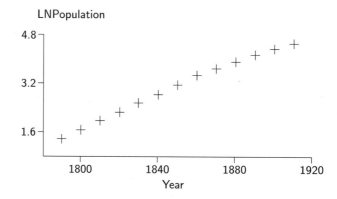

Figure 3.1   A log–lin plot of the US population data

There is a suggestion of a slight curve in the pattern formed by the points, but it looks as though it might be reasonable to fit a straight line to the plot.

Activity 3.2   Fitting a line to the transformed data

Add the regression line to the log–lin plot, and comment briefly on how well you think it represents the pattern in the plot. Use **Regression...** from the **Stats** menu to obtain the equation of the least squares fit line.

Comment

A solution is given on page 86.

Exponential functions and power laws: a reminder

You saw in Chapter C3 that a log–lin plot can be used to test for an exponential relationship and a log–log plot for a power law relationship. We include here a brief review of how these plots are used.

(1) Exponential relationship

Suppose that the relationship between two variables x and y is of the form

$$y = A \exp(bx).$$

Taking natural logarithms gives

$$\ln y = \ln(A \exp(bx))$$
$$= \ln A + \ln(\exp(bx))$$
$$= \ln A + bx,$$

that is,

$$\ln y = \ln A + bx.$$

If we write $Y = \ln y$ and $a = \ln A$, then this becomes

$$Y = a + bx,$$

which is the equation of a straight line with intercept $a = \ln A$ and gradient b. So if values of $Y = \ln y$ are plotted along the vertical axis and values of x along the horizontal axis, then the plotted points will lie along a straight line.

Conversely, if the points on a plot of $\ln y$ against x lie roughly along a straight line, then this indicates that an exponential curve is a suitable model for the relationship between y and x. If the equation of the line is $Y = a + bx$, then

$$\ln y = a + bx,$$

so

$$y = \exp(a + bx) = \exp(a)\exp(bx),$$

and $y = \exp(a)\exp(bx)$ is the equation of an exponential curve modelling the relationship between y and x. This will be illustrated in the next activity.

(2) Power law relationship

Suppose instead that the relationship between two variables x and y is of the form

$$y = Ax^b.$$

Taking natural logarithms gives

$$\begin{aligned}
\ln y &= \ln(Ax^b) \\
&= \ln A + \ln(x^b) \\
&= \ln A + b\ln x.
\end{aligned}$$

If we write $Y = \ln y$, $a = \ln A$ and $X = \ln x$, then this becomes

$$Y = a + bX,$$

which is the equation of a straight line with intercept $a = \ln A$ and gradient b. So if values of $Y = \ln y$ are plotted along the vertical axis and values of $X = \ln x$ along the horizontal axis, then the plotted points will lie along a straight line.

Conversely, if the points on a plot of $\ln y$ against $\ln x$ lie roughly along a straight line, then this indicates that a power law curve is a suitable model for the relationship between y and x. If the equation of the fit line is $Y = a + bX$, then

$$\ln y = a + b\ln x = a + \ln(x^b),$$

so

$$y = \exp(a + \ln(x^b)) = \exp(a)\exp(\ln(x^b)) = \exp(a)x^b,$$

and $y = \exp(a)x^b$ is the equation of a power law curve modelling the relationship between y and x. This will be illustrated later in this section.

Activity 3.3   Finding the equation of the fitted curve

The equation of the line you fitted to the scatterplot of LNPopulation against Year was

$$\text{LNPopulation} = -46.51 + 0.0268\,\text{Year}$$

or, replacing the capital letters LN of OUStats by the more usual ln,

$$\ln \text{Population} = -46.51 + 0.0268\,\text{Year}.$$

Rewrite this equation to obtain the equation of a curve modelling the relationship between Population and Year. Write this equation in the form $\text{Population} = \cdots$.

Comment

A solution is given on page 86.

Activity 3.4   Estimating the US population

Use the equation of the curve fitted to the US population data:

(a) to estimate the US population in 1885;

(b) to estimate the US population in 1920 and in 1950, assuming that the model for population growth remains valid beyond 1910. Comment briefly on your results.

Comment

A solution is given on page 86.

In the next two activities, you are invited to explore the relationship between the pressure of a fixed mass of gas at a fixed temperature and the volume it fills.

Activity 3.5   Transforming the data

Experimental data on the pressure of a fixed mass of gas when confined to each of six different volumes are contained in the file GAS.OUS. The volume is the explanatory variable and the pressure is the dependent variable.

(a) Obtain a scatterplot of the data.

(b) Theory suggests that volume V and pressure P should be connected by a relationship of the form

$$PV^k = C,$$

where k and C are constants. If the theory is correct, what transformation of the variables should produce a scatterplot showing a linear pattern?

Comment

A solution is given on page 87.

Activity 3.6   Fitting a curve

(a) Transform the data in the way you suggested in Activity 3.5, and obtain a scatterplot of the transformed data. Does it look as though a straight line will fit the transformed data well?

(b) Add the least squares fit line to the scatterplot of the transformed data, and obtain the equation of the line.

(c) Obtain the equation of a curve which models the relationship between the pressure of the gas and its volume. Write the equation in the form $P = \cdots$.

(d) Use the equation of the fitted curve to predict the pressure of the gas when it is confined to a volume of 120 units.

Comment

A solution is given on page 87.

Activity 3.7 Estimating the protein content of wheat

The percentage protein content of wheat varies with the yield per unit area. To investigate this relationship, data on the percentage protein content and the yield in bushels per acre were obtained for each of 19 plots. The purpose of the investigation was to find a relationship which could be used to estimate the percentage protein content of wheat for various yields.

Source: G. W. Snedecor and W. G. Cochran, *Statistical Methods* (Iowa State University Press, 7th edn, 1980).

(a) The data are in the file WHEAT.OUS. Open the file now, and obtain a scatterplot with percentage protein content along the y-axis and yield along the x-axis. Do you think a straight line would be an adequate model for the relationship?

(b) Transform the data using logarithms, and obtain a log–lin plot and a log–log plot. Display the least squares fit line on each plot. For which of these plots is a straight line a better model for the pattern in the plot?

Comment

A solution is given on page 87.

Activity 3.8 Fitting a curve

(a) Fit a straight line to the plot which you chose in part (b) of Activity 3.7. Hence obtain the equation of a curve which may be used to model the relationship between percentage protein content and yield. Write the equation in the form Protein $= \cdots$.

(b) Use your model to estimate the percentage protein content of wheat for which the yield is 12.5 bushels per acre.

Comment

A solution is given on page 88.

In this section, we have used natural logarithms (ln) to transform data. We could just as well have used logarithms to base 10 (log): the equations of the curves we fitted would have been the same (once the logs were removed), and numerical estimates using the fitted curves would have been the same. If you have the time, you might like to check this for yourself using one of the data sets from this section.

Data may be transformed in many ways using **Transform...** from the **Edit** menu. For reference, we include below a summary of how to transform data by taking natural logarithms. This is followed by a general summary of the main steps involved in transforming data, and an example to illustrate these steps.

Transforming data by taking logarithms: a summary

The data in a column of a data file may be transformed using the following steps.

◇ Choose **Transform**... from the **Edit** menu. A dialogue box for transforming variables appears; this contains a box for entering an expression, a list of variables, and a calculator keyboard.

◇ Click on the LN button on the calculator keyboard; LN appears in the **Expression to calculate** box.

◇ Select the variable name from the list on the left of the dialogue box, and click on the **Enter selected variable** button; the variable name appears in the **Expression to calculate** box enclosed in double quotes.

◇ Finally, click OK.

The transformed data are entered in the next available column. For frequency data, the frequencies are repeated in the column immediately to the right of the column containing the transformed data.

Transforming data: a summary and an example

The data in a file may be transformed using **Transform**... from the **Edit** menu. The basic steps involved are as follows.

◇ Choose **Transform**... from the **Edit** menu. A dialogue box for transforming variables appears; this contains a box for entering an expression, a list of variables, and a calculator keyboard.

◇ Enter the expression for the transformed data in the **Expression to calculate** box.

◇ Click on OK. The transformed data are entered in the next available column; this column is renamed automatically.

The expression that is entered in the **Expression to calculate** box may be any function of the variables listed that can be constructed using the keyboard in the dialogue box. Suppose, for instance, that variables named A, B and C are listed. Then expressions that may be entered include $A-B$, $A*B/C$ and LN A. Consider $A-B$, for instance; this may be entered using the following steps.

◇ Select A from the variable list on the left of the dialogue box (by clicking on it).

◇ Click on the **Enter selected variable** button located above the variable list.

◇ Click on the minus button ($-$); this is located along with other operations such as $+$ and $*$ in the centre of the dialogue box.

◇ Select B from the variable list.

◇ Click on the **Enter selected variable** button. The expression "A" $-$ "B" should now be in the **Expression to calculate** box.

◇ Click on OK. The transformed data are entered in the next available column; this column is automatically renamed $A-B$.

Appendix 1: Entering and editing data

Creating a new data file

◇ Open OUStats for MST121. Choose **New**... from the **File** menu.
You will then see a dialogue box for entering the number of rows and
columns you want to have available. It is a good idea to include a few
extra rows and columns in case you need them when you are working
with the data. Type the number of rows you require into the 'Number
of rows' box. Now move the cursor to the 'Number of columns' box by
pressing Tab (or by double-clicking on this box). Do not press Enter.
Now type in the number of columns, and then click OK or press Enter.

◇ You will then see a data window showing a data matrix of the size
you specified in the dialogue box. To enter a column of data in, say,
column V1, click in the first row of V1 and type in the first value.
Press Enter to move the cursor to the next row, and type in the next
value. Press Enter again, and continue entering values in this way.
To type in a second column of data, click in the first row of that
column and repeat the entering of values as for the first column. Note
that if you prefer to enter data across the rows rather than down the
columns, you can simply press Tab instead of Enter after typing each
value. This will move the cursor to the right.

◇ You can go back and edit any value, by clicking on it, typing in the
new value and pressing Enter. You can also move around the data
matrix using the up and down arrow keys.

Naming and renaming columns

When a new data window is selected, the default names for the columns
(that is, variables) are V1, V2, V3, etc. To rename a column, choose
Rename... from the **Edit** menu, select the original name in the dialogue
box which appears (by clicking on it), type in the new name and click OK.

Saving a new data file

Choose **Save as**... from the **File** menu. You will then see a dialogue box
for entering the name you wish to give the data file. File names may be up
to eight characters long (beginning with a letter), plus an extension. The
extension suggested in the dialogue box is .OUS. The file will be located in
the same directory as all the other data files, and it will be listed with
them when you choose **Open**... from the **File** menu.

Entering frequency data

Frequency data must be entered with the values in one column (in V1, say) and the corresponding frequencies in the next column, that is, in the column immediately to the right of the first column (in V2, in this case). To designate the values in a column as the values for frequency data, place the mouse pointer anywhere in that column and click with the *right* mouse button. Then choose 'Values with frequencies' from the menu that appears. The values in the column immediately to the right of this column will be designated as frequencies automatically. (You can check this by clicking with the right mouse button anywhere in the second column. You will notice that the values have been designated 'Frequencies'.)

When the values in two adjacent columns have been designated as 'Values with frequencies' and 'Frequencies' respectively, their variable names are linked together in dialogue boxes which display variable names. Thus, for instance, Height | Frequency refers to the frequency data which have been entered in the adjacent columns Height and Frequency.

Making your own Notes file

When you create a new data file using OUStats, it is a good idea to record information about the file (the source of the data, an explanation of the variable names, etc.) in an associated Notes file. You can do this as follows.

◇   Open the data file (if it is not already open).

◇   Click on **Notes** in the **File** menu. As there is not yet a Notes file linked to the data file, you will be presented with the warning message 'Cannot read file'; click on OK.

◇   Type your notes about the data file into the **Notes** window.

◇   To save the notes, choose **Save as**... from the **File** menu and save the file, as prompted, using the extension .TXT. For example, if the data file is named DATA.OUS, then save the associated Notes file as DATA.TXT.

The commands **Cut**, **Copy**, **Paste**, **Undo** and **Clear** in the **Edit** menu are available whenever a Notes window is open.

Transferring data into and out of OUStats

Instructions for transferring data from Mathcad (or another application) into OUStats or vice versa are given in the OUStats Help file, which may be accessed via the OUStats **Help** menu.

Appendix 2: The data files

A brief description of the data in each data file included with the OUStats software is given below. For more detailed information on a data file, you should refer to the **Notes** file which accompanies it.

ages.ous

The data in this file are the ages, in months, of 113 students enrolled on an elementary statistics course.

Source: B. W. Lindgren and D. A. Berry, *Elementary Statistics* (Macmillan, 1981) page 67.

alloys.ous

Data are given on the iron content of 13 specimens of cupro-nickel alloys, and the weight loss of each specimen when tested for corrosion.

Source: N. R. Draper and W. L. Smith, *Applied Regression Analysis* (John Wiley, 1966) page 37.

apples.ous

This file contains the number of apples produced by each of 12 apple trees, and the percentage of fruit on each tree attacked by codling moth larvae.

Source: G. W. Snedecor and W. G. Cochran, *Statistical Methods* (Iowa State University Press, 7th edn, 1980) page 162.

austen.ous

This data file contains the lengths of 60 sentences from *Sense and Sensibility* by Jane Austen. Sentences were chosen by two different methods, 30 using each method.

Source: The data were collected by C. E. Graham in 1996.

authors.ous

The data are the lengths of a large sample of sentences from each of three books, one by each of H. G. Wells, G. K. Chesterton and G. B. Shaw.

Source: C. B. Williams, 'A note on the statistical analysis of sentence length as a criterion of literary style', *Biometrika* 31 (1940) pages 356–361.

bar.ous

The data in this file are the gross hourly earnings, in pence, in 1995, of 14 female bar staff.

bearings.ous

This file contains the diameters, in millimetres, of 60 ball-bearings produced by a company.

Source: M. R. Spiegel, *Statistics*, Schaum's Outline Series (McGraw-Hill, 1972) page 43.

bears.ous

This data file contains the results of aerial surveys carried out on each of 20 days in a particular part of Alaska. The average wind speed and the number of black bears sighted on each day are given.

Source: B. W. Lindgren and D. A. Berry, *Elementary Statistics* (Macmillan, 1981) page 137.

birds.ous

This data file contains the weights (in grams) and the wing lengths (in mm) of a sample of grasshopper warblers in Fineshade Woods, Northamptonshire, and the wing lengths (in mm) of two samples of sand-martins (adults and juveniles) at a quarry near Wansford, Cambridgeshire.

Source: The data are from the notebook of B. P. Galpin (an ornithologist), and are based on two bird studies carried out during 1995–96.

birthwt.ous

The data are the birthweights, to the nearest gram, of 71 babies (boys and girls) who were all born two weeks early, that is, at the end of a 38-week gestation period.

blackcap.ous

The data are the weights (in grams) of two samples of blackcaps, one obtained in July 1994 and the other in September 1994, just prior to migration.

Source: The data were supplied by N. J. Phillips.

brothers.ous

This file contains data on the heights of 1401 brother–sister pairs. The heights of the brothers are listed separately for sisters of different heights. These data are also contained in the file *siblings.ous*, but they are arranged differently there. The data were collected in the 1890s as part of an investigation into the inheritance of physical characteristics.

Source: K. Pearson and A. Lee, 'On the laws of inheritance in man', *Biometrika* 2 (1903) pages 357–462.

build.ous

The data in this file are the heights, in inches, and weights, in pounds, of 98 students (53 men and 45 women) following an elementary statistics course (in the USA).

Source: B. W. Lindgren and D. A. Berry, *Elementary Statistics* (Macmillan, 1981) pages 510–512.

castings.ous

This file contains data on the breaking stresses (in tons per square inch) of a sample of large castings and of test-pieces produced at the same time as the castings.

Source: G. B. Wetherill, *Intermediate Statistical Methods* (Chapman and Hall, 1981) page 31.

chol1.ous

This file contains data on the blood cholesterol measurements (in mg per 100 ml) of two groups of heavy middle-aged men.

Source: S. Selvin, *Statistical Analysis of Epidemiological Data* (Oxford University Press, 1991) Table 2.1.

chol2.ous

This file contains data on the blood cholesterol levels (in mg per dl) of 28 patients two days and four days after suffering a heart attack, and of 30 people who had not had a heart attack.

Source: B. F. Ryan, B. L. Joiner and T. A. Ryan, *Minitab Handbook* (PWS Publishers, 1985) page 93.

cigars.ous

This file contains data on the US production of small cigars for each year from 1945 to 1954.

Source: M. R. Spiegel, *Statistics*, Schaum's Outline Series (McGraw-Hill, 1972) page 233.

concrete.ous

The speed (in km per second) at which an ultrasonic pulse passes through concrete and the crushing strength (in newtons per square mm) of the concrete are given for 14 samples of concrete.

Source: The data are adapted from an example described in J. T. Callender and R. Jackson, *Probability and Statistics with Spreadsheets* (Prentice Hall, 1995).

couples.ous

This file contains data on the heights of 1079 father–mother pairs. The data were collected in the 1890s as part of an investigation into the inheritance of physical characteristics.

Source: K. Pearson and A. Lee, 'On the laws of inheritance in man', *Biometrika* 2 (1903) pages 357–462.

cricket.ous

This file contains the number of runs scored in each innings in 1996 by two cricketers who played in the same teams at under-15 club and county level.

criminal.ous

This file contains the heights of 3000 criminals and 1000 Cambridge men in 1902. The data were collected as part of a study to compare various physical measurements for criminals and for the rest of the population.

Source: W. R. MacDonell, 'On criminal anthropometry and the identification of criminals', *Biometrika* 1 (1902) pages 177–227.

cuckoos.ous

This data file contains the lengths, measured to the nearest half millimetre, of 243 cuckoo eggs.

Source: O. H. Latter, 'The egg of *Cuculus canorus*', *Biometrika* 1 (1902) pages 164–176.

cuckoos2.ous

This data file contains the breadths, measured to the nearest half millimetre, of 243 cuckoo eggs.

Source: O. H. Latter, 'The egg of *Cuculus canorus*', *Biometrika* 1 (1902) pages 164–176.

daughter.ous

This file contains data on the heights of 1375 mother–daughter pairs. The heights of daughters are listed separately for mothers of different heights. The data were collected in the 1890s as part of an investigation into the inheritance of physical characteristics.

Source: K. Pearson and A. Lee, 'On the laws of inheritance in man', *Biometrika* 2 (1903) pages 357–462.

decay.ous

This file contains data on the amount of radioactivity remaining in a sample of radioactive material after various lengths of time.

Source: M101 (Mathematics: A Foundation Course), Block V, Unit 1.

dipper.ous

This file contains the weights, in grams, of 198 Irish dipper nestlings aged 6–8 days.

Source: J. O'Halloran, P. Smiddy and B. O'Mahony, 'Biometrics, growth and sex ratios amongst Irish Dippers', *Ringing and Migration* 13 (1992) pages 152–161.

dter3.ous

This file contains data on the heights of 1376 father–daughter pairs. The heights of daughters are listed separately for fathers of different heights. These data are also given in *pearson3.ous*, but they are arranged differently there. The data were collected in the 1890s as part of an investigation into the inheritance of physical characteristics.

Source: K. Pearson and A. Lee, 'On the laws of inheritance in man', *Biometrika* 2 (1903) pages 357–462.

faithful.ous

Data are given on the durations of eruptions and the intervals between eruptions of the Old Faithful geyser in Yellowstone National Park, Wyoming, USA, in August 1978.

Source: M246, *Elements of Statistics*, page 36.

fat.ous

The age, in years, and the body fat percentage are given for 14 women.

Source: R. B. Mazess, W. W. Peppler and M. Gibbons, 'Total body composition by dual-photon absorptiometry', *American Journal of Clinical Nutrition* 40 (1984) pages 834–839.

fathers.ous

This file contains data on the heights of 1079 father–mother pairs. The heights of the fathers are listed separately for mothers of different heights. These data are also contained in *couples.ous*, but they are arranged differently there. The data were collected in the 1890s as part of an investigation into the inheritance of physical characteristics.

Source: K. Pearson and A. Lee, 'On the laws of inheritance in man', *Biometrika* 2 (1903) pages 357–462.

fibrin.ous

Information is given on the level of fibrin in the blood at various times after a substance (not named in the source) is injected into the bloodstream.

Source: The data are adapted from an example in G. B. Wetherill, *Intermediate Statistical Methods* (Chapman and Hall, 1981).

fish.ous

The data are the lengths, in millimetres, of 20 fish, and the lengths of their otoliths (ear stones).

Source: J. Fowler and L. Cohen, *Statistics for Ornithologists* (British Trust for Ornithology, 1988) page 106.

flies.ous

This file contains data on the mean number of eggs laid per day during the first fourteen days of life for 25 females of each of three genetic lines of the fruitfly *Drosophila melanogaster*.

Source: R. R. Sokal and F. J. Rohlf, *Biometry* (W. H. Freeman, 2nd edn, 1981) page 239.

gas.ous

The data are experimental values of the pressure of a fixed mass of gas when filling various volumes.

Source: M. R. Spiegel, *Statistics*, Schaum's Outline Series (McGraw-Hill, 1972) page 235.

geyser.ous

The lengths are given of 299 intervals between successive eruptions of the Old Faithful geyser between 1 August 1985 and 15 August 1985. (The Old Faithful geyser is a tourist attraction in Yellowstone National Park, Wyoming, USA.)

Source: A. Azzalini and A. W. Bowman, 'A look at some data on the Old Faithful geyser', *Applied Statistics* 39 (1990) pages 357–363.

heights.ous

The data are the heights of 1000 Cambridge men in 1902.

Source: W. R. MacDonell, 'On criminal anthropometry and the identification of criminals', *Biometrika* 1 (1902) pages 177–227.

iq.ous

Information is given on the intelligence of 112 children. Intelligence was measured using the Stanford Revision of the Simon-Binet Intelligence Scale.

Source: L. M. Terman, *The Intelligence of School Children* (Houghton Mifflin, 1919).

islands.ous

This file contains the areas, in hectares, of 11 small islands in the Shetland Islands, and the number of breeding bird species on each island.

Source: J. Fowler and L. Cohen, *Statistics for Ornithologists* (British Trust for Ornithology, 1988) page 114.

laurel.ous

This file contains the lengths, recorded to the nearest millimetre, of 40 laurel leaves.

Source: M. R. Spiegel, *Statistics*, Schaum's Outline Series (McGraw-Hill, 1972) page 35.

means.ous

The data are the mean heights of sons for fathers of different heights. The means were calculated from the data in *sons.ous*.

means2.ous

The data are the mean heights of daughters for mothers of different heights. The means were calculated from the data in *daughter.ous*.

means3.ous

The data are the mean heights of daughters for fathers of different heights, and the mean heights of sons for mothers of different heights. The means were calculated from the data in *dter3.ous* and *sons3.ous*.

means4.ous

The data are the mean heights of fathers for mothers of different heights, and the mean heights of mothers for fathers of different heights. The means were calculated from the data in *fathers.ous* and *mothers.ous*.

means5.ous

The data are the mean heights of sisters for brothers of different heights, and the mean heights of brothers for sisters of different heights. The means were calculated from the data in *brothers.ous* and *sisters.ous*.

memory.ous

The scores and memorisation times are given for two groups of people, one young and one elderly, who took part in a test of spatial memory.

Source: The data were collected between September 1989 and August 1992 as part of the PhD project of Jennifer Day (Department of Psychology, University of Sheffield).

mothers.ous

This file contains data on the heights of 1079 father–mother pairs. The heights of the mothers are listed separately for fathers of different heights. These data are also given in *couples.ous*, but they are arranged differently there. The data were collected in the 1890s as part of an investigation into the inheritance of physical characteristics.

Source: K. Pearson and A. Lee, 'On the laws of inheritance in man', *Biometrika* 2 (1903) pages 357–462.

pearson.ous

This file contains data on the heights of 1078 father–son pairs. The data were collected in the 1890s as part of an investigation into the inheritance of physical characteristics.

Source: K. Pearson and A. Lee, 'On the laws of inheritance in man', *Biometrika* 2 (1903) pages 357–462.

pearson2.ous

This file contains data on the heights of 1375 mother–daughter pairs. The data were collected in the 1890s as part of an investigation into the inheritance of physical characteristics.

Source: K. Pearson and A. Lee, 'On the laws of inheritance in man', *Biometrika* 2 (1903) pages 357–462.

pearson3.ous

This file contains data on the heights of 1376 father–daughter pairs and 1057 mother–son pairs. The data were collected in the 1890s as part of an investigation into the inheritance of physical characteristics.

Source: K. Pearson and A. Lee, 'On the laws of inheritance in man', *Biometrika* 2 (1903) pages 357–462.

pipits.ous

The wing lengths of 31 male and 27 female meadow pipits are given, to the nearest millimetre.

plants.ous

This data file contains the area (in km^2) of each of 30 islands in the Galápagos Archipelago, and the number of plant species observed on each island.

Source: M. P. Johnson and P. H. Raven, 'Species number and endemism: the Galápagos Archipelago revisited', *Science* 179 (1973) pages 893–895.

primary.ous

The data are the gross weekly earnings (in pounds) in 1995 of 37 male and 54 female primary school teachers.

pulse.ous

The data in this file are the pulse rates of a group of students. They were collected in a classroom experiment by Brian Joiner. The pulse data are listed in several ways: for example, for males and females separately, and for smokers and non-smokers separately.

Source: B. F. Ryan, B. L. Joiner and T. A. Ryan, *Minitab Handbook* (PWS Publishers, 1985) pages 319–321.

radial.ous

This file contains data on the radial velocities (in kilometres per second) of 80 stars in a small region of the sky. The data are grouped.

Source: R. J. Trumple and H. F. Weaver, *Statistical Astronomy* (University of California Press, 1953) page 194.

rainfall.ous

This file contains 30 successive values of the March rainfall (in inches) for Minneapolis/St Paul in the USA.

Source: D. Hinkley, 'On quick choice of power transformation', *Applied Statistics* 26 (1977) pages 67–69.

rats.ous

This file contains the total lengths of life (in days) of two groups of rats. One group was put on a restricted diet after an initial weaning period, and the other was put on a free-eating diet.

Source: R. L. Berger, D. D. Boos and F. M. Guess, 'Test and confidence sets for comparing two mean residual life functions', *Biometrics* 44 (1988) pages 103–115.

run.ous

The data in this file are the pulse rates of a group of 35 students before and immediately after running in place for one minute. They were collected in a classroom experiment by Brian Joiner. The pulse data are listed in several ways: for example, for males and females separately, and for smokers and non-smokers separately.

Source: B. F. Ryan, B. L. Joiner and T. A. Ryan, *Minitab Handbook* (PWS Publishers, 1985) pages 319–321.

siblings.ous

This file contains data on the heights of 328 brother–brother pairs, 473 sister–sister pairs and 1401 brother–sister pairs. The data were collected in the 1890s as part of an investigation into the inheritance of physical characteristics.

Source: K. Pearson and A. Lee, 'On the laws of inheritance in man', *Biometrika* 2 (1903) pages 357–462.

sisters.ous

This file contains data on the heights of 1401 brother–sister pairs. The heights of the sisters are listed separately for brothers of different heights. These data are also contained in the file *siblings.ous*, but they are arranged differently there. The data were collected in the 1890s as part of an investigation into the inheritance of physical characteristics.

Source: K. Pearson and A. Lee, 'On the laws of inheritance in man', *Biometrika* 2 (1903) pages 357–462.

skua.ous

The data consist of the mean wing lengths of a group of ducks at various ages.

Source: J. Fowler and L. Cohen, *Statistics for Ornithologists* (British Trust for Ornithology, 1988) page 113.

snowfall.ous

The annual snowfall (in inches) in Buffalo, NY, is given for each year from 1910 to 1972.

Source: E. Parzen, 'Nonparametric statistical data modelling', *Journal of the American Statistical Association* 74 (1979) pages 105–131.

sons.ous

This file contains data on the heights of 1078 father–son pairs. The heights of the sons are listed separately for fathers of different heights. The data were collected in the 1890s as part of an investigation into the inheritance of physical characteristics.

Source: K. Pearson and A. Lee, 'On the laws of inheritance in man', *Biometrika* 2 (1903) pages 357–462.

sons3.ous

This file contains data on the heights of 1057 mother–son pairs. The heights of the sons are listed separately for mothers of different heights. These data are also given in *pearson3.ous*, but they are arranged differently there. The data were collected in the 1890s as part of an investigation into the inheritance of physical characteristics.

Source: K. Pearson and A. Lee, 'On the laws of inheritance in man', *Biometrika* 2 (1903) pages 357–462.

speed.ous

This file contains the average speed, in miles per hour, of the winner of the Indianapolis 500 auto race for each year between 1962 and 1971 (inclusive).

Source: G. W. Snedecor and W. G. Cochran, *Statistical Methods* (Iowa State University Press, 7th edn, 1980) page 152.

stamps.ous

The data consist of the percentage success rates for next-day delivery of letters for various countries, and the price of a standard letter (in pence) for each country.

Source: *The Observer*, Business Section, 9 June 1996, page 5, and OECD data.

stars.ous

This data file contains data on the absolute magnitude and surface temperature (in degrees Kelvin) of 48 stars in the Milky Way. Data are included for some supergiants, giants and main sequence stars.

uspop.ous

This file contains data on the population of the USA, in millions, at ten-year intervals from 1790 to 1910 inclusive.

Source: M101 (Mathematics: A Foundation Course), Block II, Unit 1.

uspop2.ous

This file contains data on the population of the USA, in millions, at ten-year intervals from 1790 to 1960 inclusive.

Source: M101 (Mathematics: A Foundation Course), Block II, Unit 1, and US Bureau of the Census.

warbler.ous

The data in this file are the wing lengths (in mm) of 70 willow warblers, measured between April and July 1994.

Source: The data were supplied by N. J. Phillips.

wheat.ous

The yield of wheat, in bushels per acre, is given for each of 19 plots, together with the percentage protein content of wheat from the plots.

Source: G. W. Snedecor and W. G. Cochran, *Statistical Methods* (Iowa State University Press, 7th edn, 1980) page 399.

wheatear.ous

This data file contains the wing lengths of male and female migrant wheatears caught in the spring seasons of 1970–1989 as they passed through Bardsey, Gwynedd.

Source: P. Hope Jones, 'Wing lengths and weights of spring Wheatears *Oenanthe oenanthe* at Bardsey, Gwynedd', *Ringing and Migration* 13 (1992) pages 162–166.

worldpop.ous

These data are World Bank estimates for the population of the Earth in various years. These data are explored using Mathcad in Block C, Chapter C3.

Appendix 3: Using StatsAid

To run *StatsAid* in *Windows 3.1*, double-click on the **StatsAid** icon in the **MST121 Block D** window. In *Windows 95*, click on the **Start** menu, move the mouse pointer to **Programs**, then to **MST121 Block D**, and finally click on **StatsAid**.

The following list of topics is displayed on the opening screen.

Frequency diagrams
The median and quartiles
Boxplots
The mean
Standard deviation
Scatterplots

This screen is called the exercise map. Each of these six topics has 2, 3 or 4 exercises, indicated by the number of square boxes on the screen to the right of the topic names. To run an exercise on a topic, click on the topic name and then click OK.

Although you can study any individual exercise on its own (by clicking on its box), you are recommended to start at the first exercise for a given topic and be guided through each exercise in turn.

You can return to the exercise map at any time, using the **Exercises** menu. The exercise map can be used to review your progress and select another topic or exercise.

Across the top left of the screen are the five menus; these are explained below.

File contains the **Exit** command, which is used to exit from StatsAid.

Exercises contains five commands.

◇ **Exercise map** shows the top-level screen of StatsAid, lists the six topics, and summarises your progress through the various exercises in the package.

◇ **Reset progress record**, when selected, allows you to delete the record of your progress through the package.

◇ **Previous exercise** (**Pg up**) returns you to the previous exercise in the package. The same result is achieved by pressing Page Up on the keyboard.

◇ **Repeat exercise** allows you to repeat the exercise you are currently using.

◇ **Next exercise** (**Pg down**) allows you to move on to the next exercise in the package. The same result is achieved by pressing Page Down on the keyboard.

Options contains two commands.

◇ **Change text size** allows you to select either standard or large text size.

◇ **Change colour scheme** allows you to change the colours displayed when the package is running. Four colour combinations are available. Each time this command is selected, the next combination in the sequence is chosen. You can select this command several times until you find a colour combination you like. (This feature is not available if you are using a sixteen-colour display.)

Tools contains two commands.

◇ **Calculator** displays the calculator which is resident on your computer's operating system. Note that this calculator itself contains drop-down menus; these are explained in your computer literature.

◇ **Paste (Ctrl + V)** pastes the contents of the clipboard to the current cursor position. For example, you can copy a result displayed in the calculator (using the calculator's Copy command) and paste it into a solution box of one of the exercises.

Help contains one command, **About StatsAid**, which states the current version of the package.

Appendix 4: Optional Mathcad files

Please note that looking at these files is entirely optional. The computer activities for this block do not make use of Mathcad.

121D1-01   Random numbers and probability simulations

121D2-01   Summary statistics and bar charts

121D2-02   Using data files within Mathcad
(There are two data files, bar.prn and cuckoos.prn to accompany this document.)

121D2-03   Exploring normal curves

121D3-01   Calculating a confidence interval

121D4-01   Performing a two-sample z-test

121D5-01   Fitting lines and curves to data

Solutions to Activities

Chapter D2

Solution 3.2

Frequency diagrams for the four data sets are shown in Figure S2.1.

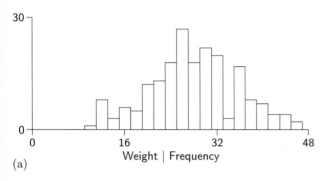

(a)

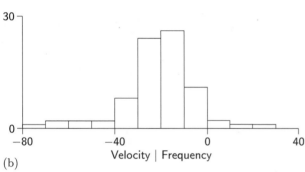

(b)

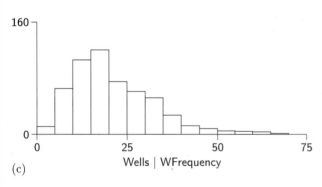

(c)

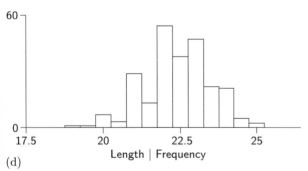

(d)

Figure S2.1 Four frequency diagrams

(a) The first frequency diagram (for the weights of Irish dipper nestlings) was obtained using the first interval starting value and interval width suggested in the activity (9 and 2, respectively).

(b) For the frequency diagram for the radial velocities, a first interval starting value of −80 and an interval width of 10 were used, corresponding to the grouping of the data.

(c) To obtain the frequency diagram for the lengths of sentences written by H. G. Wells, a first interval starting value of 0.5 and a width of 5 were used. This means that the first bar represents sentences of lengths 1 to 5 inclusive, the second bar represents sentences of lengths 6 to 10 inclusive, and so on. You may well have chosen different values for the start of the first interval and the interval width.

(d) The lengths of cuckoo eggs are given to the nearest half millimetre, so a length recorded as 19 mm could be anywhere between 18.75 mm and 19.25 mm. To obtain the frequency diagram shown, a first interval starting value of 18.75 and an interval width of 0.5 were used.

The frequency diagram for the lengths of sentences written by H. G. Wells is right-skewed (the right tail is longer than the left tail), so a normal distribution is not an appropriate model in this case. The other three frequency diagrams are all roughly symmetrical with a single clear peak, so a normal model is worth considering for these data. You are asked to investigate these three data sets further in the next three activities.

Solution 3.4

I fitted a normal model with mean −21 and standard deviation 16. (As in Activity 3.3, I used one significant figure more for the parameters of the normal distribution than are given in the data.)

The four frequency diagrams I obtained are shown in Figure S2.2. (The size of each random sample was 80, the same as the size of the sample of data.)

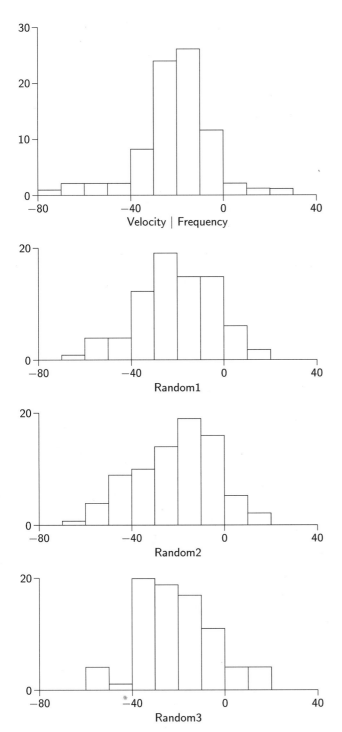

Figure S2.2 Four frequency diagrams

As you can see, there is considerable variation between the shapes of the frequency diagrams for the random samples. However, they all appear to be less sharply peaked than the frequency diagram for the data, which has longer shallower tails. It would appear that a normal model may not be a very good fit for the data. Certainly, the fit does not seem to be as good in this case as the fit of the normal curve to the weights of Irish dipper nestlings in Activity 3.3.

Solution 3.5

I fitted a normal distribution with mean 22.4 and standard deviation 1.08. (Again, I used one significant figure more for the parameters of the normal distribution than are given in the data.)

The four frequency diagrams I obtained are shown in Figure S2.3. (The size of each random sample was 243, the same as the size of the sample of data.)

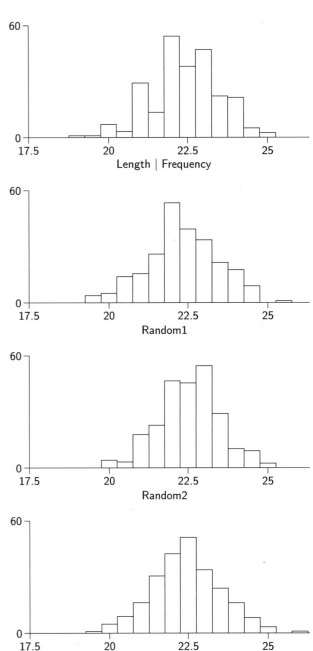

Figure S2.3 Four frequency diagrams

Again, there is considerable variation between the shapes of the frequency diagrams for the random samples. The main difference between the frequency diagram for the data and the frequency diagrams for the random samples is that the frequency diagram for the data is more jagged. Apart from this, the fit seems to be quite good.

Chapter D2

Solution 5.1

All the areas are equal to 0.683.

Solution 5.2

(a) All the areas are equal to 0.683.

(b) The area under a normal curve from one standard deviation below the mean to one standard deviation above the mean is the same whatever the mean and standard deviation of the distribution. That is, the proportion of values within one standard deviation of the mean is 68.3% for any normal distribution.

Solution 5.3

(a) All the areas are equal to 0.954.

(b) The area under a normal curve from two standard deviations below the mean to two standard deviations above the mean is the same whatever the mean and standard deviation of the distribution. That is, the proportion of values within two standard deviations of the mean is 95.4% for any normal distribution.

Solution 5.4

In this case, all the areas are equal to 0.997.

The area under a normal curve from three standard deviations below the mean to three standard deviations above the mean is the same whatever the mean and standard deviation of the distribution. That is, the proportion of values within three standard deviations of the mean is 99.7% for any normal distribution.

Solution 5.5

(a) The area to the left of 1.644 85 is 0.95, so the area between $-1.644\,85$ and $1.644\,85$ is equal to 0.9. The required value is $z = 1.644\,85$.

(b) The area under the normal curve between

$$\mu - z\sigma = 20 - 1.644\,85 \times 5 = 11.775\,75$$

and

$$\mu + z\sigma = 20 + 1.644\,85 \times 5 = 28.224\,25$$

is equal to 0.9.

(c) Whatever values of μ and σ you choose, you should find that the area under the normal curve between $\mu - 1.644\,85\sigma$ and $\mu + 1.644\,85\sigma$ is equal to 0.9.

(d) The area under a normal curve within 1.644 85 standard deviations of the mean is 0.9, whatever the values of the mean and standard deviation.

In practice, we shall normally use the value of z calculated to only 3 significant figures (which is 2 decimal places in this case). Rounding to 2 decimal places gives 1.64, and this is the value that is commonly used; we do not usually require greater accuracy than this. So we have the following result.

For a population modelled by a normal distribution with mean μ and standard deviation σ, approximately 90% of the population are within 1.64 standard deviations of the mean, that is, between $\mu - 1.64\sigma$ and $\mu + 1.64\sigma$.

Solution 5.6

(a) If the area between $-z$ and z is equal to 0.95, then the area of each tail is $\frac{1}{2} \times 0.05 = 0.025$. So the total area to the left of z is 0.975. This is illustrated in Figure S2.4.

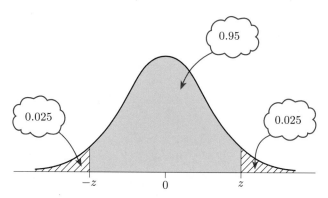

(a) The area between $-z$ and z

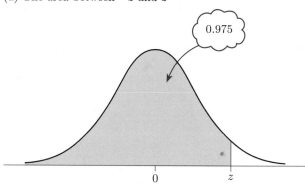

(b) The area to the left of z

Figure S2.4   Finding the area to the left of z

The area to the left of 1.959 96 is equal to 0.975. The required value is $z = 1.959\,96$.

(b) The area under the normal curve between

$$\mu - z\sigma = 20 - 1.959\,96 \times 5 = 10.2002$$

and

$$\mu + z\sigma = 20 + 1.959\,96 \times 5 = 29.7998$$

is equal to 0.95.

(c) Whatever values of μ and σ you choose, you should find that the area under the normal curve between $\mu - 1.959\,96\sigma$ and $\mu + 1.959\,96\sigma$ is equal to 0.95.

(d) The area under a normal curve within $1.959\,96 \simeq 1.96$ standard deviations of the mean is 0.95, whatever the values of the mean and standard deviation.

For a population modelled by a normal distribution with mean μ and standard deviation σ, approximately 95% of the population are within 1.96 standard deviations of the mean, that is, between $\mu - 1.96\sigma$ and $\mu + 1.96\sigma$.

Solution 5.7

(a) If the area between $-z$ and z is equal to 0.99, then the area of each tail is $\frac{1}{2} \times 0.01 = 0.005$. So the total area to the left of z is 0.995. This is illustrated in Figure S2.5.

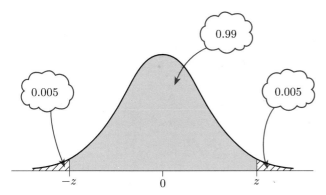

(a) The area between $-z$ and z

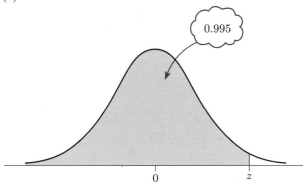

(b) The area to the left of z

Figure S2.5 Finding the area to the left of z

For the area to the left of z to be 0.995, z must be equal to 2.575 83.

(b) The area under the normal curve between

$$\mu - z\sigma = 20 - 2.575\,83 \times 5 = 7.120\,85$$

and

$$\mu + z\sigma = 20 + 2.575\,83 \times 5 = 32.879\,15$$

is equal to 0.99.

(c) Whatever values of μ and σ you choose, you should find that the area under the normal curve between $\mu - 2.575\,83\sigma$ and $\mu + 2.575\,83\sigma$ is equal to 0.99.

(d) The area under a normal curve within $2.575\,83 \simeq 2.58$ standard deviations of the mean is 0.99, whatever the values of the mean and standard deviation.

For a population modelled by a normal distribution with mean μ and standard deviation σ, approximately 99% of the population are within 2.58 standard deviations of the mean, that is, between $\mu - 2.58\sigma$ and $\mu + 2.58\sigma$.

Chapter D3

Solution 3.5

The 95% confidence interval for the mean length (in millimetres) of cuckoo eggs given by OUStats is $(22.28, 22.55)$. So, rounding to 3 significant figures, a 95% confidence interval for the mean length (in millimetres) of cuckoo eggs is $(22.3, 22.6)$.

Solution 3.6

(a) Frequency diagrams of sentence lengths for each of the three authors are shown in Figure S3.1. In each case, a first interval starting value of 0.5 and an interval width of 5 was used. In order to produce these diagrams, which all have similar scales, I had to use **Tile** from the **Window** menu and then adjust the sizes of the windows by dragging the mouse.

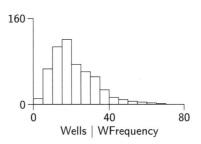

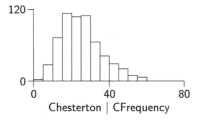

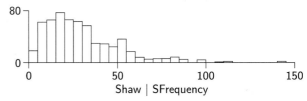

Figure S3.1 Frequency diagrams of sentence lengths

The sentence lengths from the book by Shaw are much more variable than the sentence lengths from either of the other two books. There are more long sentences, and some very long ones.

(b) The mean sentence lengths for Wells, Chesterton and Shaw are (according to OUStats) 21.68, 25.61 and 31.16 respectively; that is, approximately 21.7, 25.6 and 31.2. So, on average, Shaw seems to have written the longest sentences and Wells the shortest.

(c) The 95% confidence intervals for the mean sentence lengths in each of the three books, as given by OUStats, are as follows.

Wells	$(20.74, 22.62)$
Chesterton	$(24.75, 26.48)$
Shaw	$(29.45, 32.88)$

Rounding the confidence limits to 3 significant figures (one more than is given in the data) gives the following.

Wells	$(20.7, 22.6)$
Chesterton	$(24.8, 26.5)$
Shaw	$(29.5, 32.9)$

These confidence intervals are represented in the sketch in Figure S3.2.

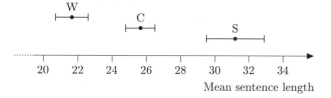

Figure S3.2   Confidence intervals

Since these confidence intervals do not overlap, this suggests that the mean sentence lengths in the books are different. It looks as though the mean sentence length in the book by Shaw is greater than the mean sentence length in the book by Chesterton, and that this is in turn greater than the mean sentence length in the book by Wells.

However, we cannot say how confident we are that the means are different. For instance, although we are 95% confident that the mean length of sentences in the book by Wells is between 20.7 and 22.6, and we are 95% confident that the mean length of sentences in the book by Chesterton is between 24.8 and 26.5, we cannot put a figure to our confidence that the two means are different: this might be more or less than 95%, but we cannot say what it is simply by comparing the two 95% confidence intervals.

If we want to be able to quantify our confidence that the means are different, then a different approach is needed; a method which compares the two samples of data is required, rather than a method which looks at each sample separately. Such a method is discussed in the next chapter.

Solution 3.7

The 95% confidence intervals for the mean birthweights of boys and girls born two weeks early, as given by OUStats, are as follows.

| Boys | $(3068, 3350)$ |
| Girls | $(2912, 3239)$ |

These confidence intervals are represented in the sketch in Figure S3.3.

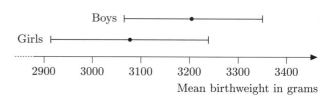

Figure S3.3   Confidence intervals

Although the confidence limits are higher for the boys than for the girls, the two intervals overlap, so we cannot draw conclusions from these confidence intervals about whether there is a difference between the mean birthweights of boys and girls born two weeks early.

Chapter D4

Solution 2.4

Boxplots of the men's and women's earnings are shown in Figure S4.1.

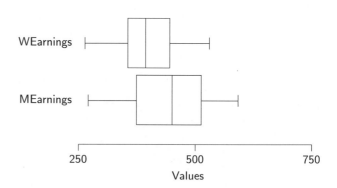

Figure S4.1   Gross weekly earnings (in pounds) of male and female primary school teachers

The earnings of the men seem to be generally higher than the earnings of the women, although the difference does not appear to be great. The difference is greatest for the highest earners in the two groups, and is very small for the lowest earners in the two groups.

Chapter D4

Solution 4.3

(a) The boxplots are shown in Figure S4.2.

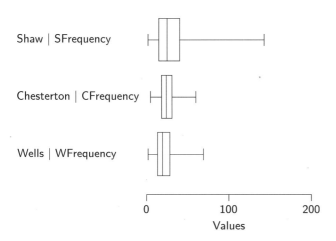

Figure S4.2 Boxplots of sentence lengths

As you can see, all the books contained quite a high proportion of fairly short sentences; and all three boxplots are right-skewed, indicating that long sentences are less common than shorter ones in all three books. The main difference between the sentence lengths in the three samples seems to be that some of the sentences in the book by Shaw are longer than any of the sentences in the samples from the other two books. The average sentence length, as measured by the median, is longest for the sample from the book by Shaw and shortest for the sample from the book by Wells.

(b) The null and alternative hypotheses may be written as

$$H_0 : \mu_C = \mu_W,$$
$$H_1 : \mu_C \neq \mu_W,$$

where μ_C is the mean sentence length in the book by G. K. Chesterton and μ_W is the mean sentence length in the book by H. G. Wells.

The test statistic (obtained from OUStats) is $z = 6.054$.

Since the test statistic $z = 6.054 > 1.96$, we reject the null hypothesis at the 5% significance level in favour of the alternative hypothesis. We conclude that the mean sentence length in the book by Chesterton is not equal to the mean sentence length in the book by Wells. The sample mean is greater for the book by Chesterton than for the book by Wells, so this suggests that the mean sentence length is greater for the book by Chesterton than for the book by Wells.

(c) The null and alternative hypotheses may be written as

$$H_0 : \mu_C = \mu_S,$$
$$H_1 : \mu_C \neq \mu_S,$$

where μ_C is the mean sentence length in the book by G. K. Chesterton and μ_S is the mean sentence length in the book by G. B. Shaw.

The test statistic (obtained from OUStats) is $z = -5.674$.

Since the test statistic $z = -5.674 < -1.96$, we reject the null hypothesis at the 5% significance level in favour of the alternative hypothesis. We conclude that the mean sentence length in the book by Chesterton is not equal to the mean sentence length in the book by Shaw. The sample mean is greater for the book by Shaw than for the book by Chesterton, so this suggests that the mean sentence length is greater for the book by Shaw than for the book by Chesterton.

Solution 4.4

(a) The boxplots are shown in Figure S4.3.

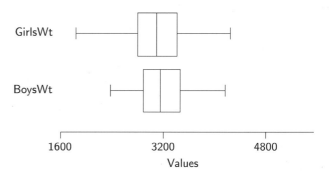

Figure S4.3 Boxplots of birthweights

No great difference is apparent between the birthweights of the boys and the girls, although the median birthweight is slightly higher for the boys than for the girls, and there is less spread in the boys' birthweights.

(b) The null and alternative hypotheses may be written as

$$H_0 : \mu_B = \mu_G,$$
$$H_1 : \mu_B \neq \mu_G,$$

where μ_B is the mean birthweight of baby boys born two weeks early and μ_G is the mean birthweight of baby girls born two weeks early.

The test statistic (obtained from OUStats) is $z = 1.21$.

Since $-1.96 < z < 1.96$, we cannot reject the null hypothesis at the 5% significance level. There is no evidence at the 5% significance level to suggest that the mean birthweight of boys born two weeks early is different from the mean birthweight of girls born two weeks early.

Solution 4.5

The null and alternative hypotheses may be written as

$$H_0 : \mu_M = \mu_F,$$
$$H_1 : \mu_M \neq \mu_F,$$

where μ_M is the mean gross weekly earnings in pounds of male primary school teachers in 1995 and μ_F is the mean gross weekly earnings of female primary school teachers in 1995.

The test statistic (obtained from OUStats) is $z = 2.79$.

Since the test statistic $z = 2.79 > 1.96$, we reject the null hypothesis at the 5% significance level in favour of the alternative hypothesis. We conclude that there was a difference between the mean gross weekly earnings in 1995 of male and female primary school teachers. The sample mean is greater for the men than for the women, so this suggests that the mean gross weekly earnings of male primary school teachers in 1995 was greater than the mean gross weekly earnings of female primary school teachers in 1995.

Chapter D5

Solution 2.2

(a) The scatterplot and the least squares fit line are shown in Figure S5.1. Note that each 'plus' on the scatterplot may represent the heights of one father–son pair or of many pairs: it is not possible to tell how many, as frequencies are not represented. If you feel that the line shown does not look as if it is the best fit line, then this is probably because when looking at the scatterplot you cannot take into account the relative frequencies of the different pairs of values.

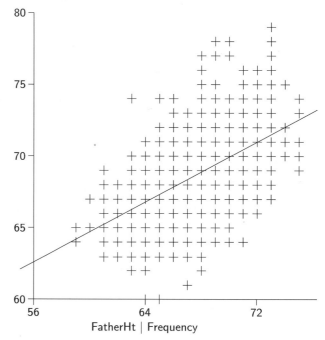

Figure S5.1   A scatterplot of son's height against father's height

(b) The equation of the least squares fit line is

$$y = 33.69 + 0.5169x,$$

where y represents son's height and x represents father's height.

The predicted height of the son of a 70-inch-tall man is

$$y = 33.69 + 0.5169 \times 70 \simeq 69.9 \text{ inches.}$$

However, the data on which the model is based were collected in the 1890s for fathers and sons in the UK. If the average height of men has continued to increase from generation to generation, possibly by different amounts in different generations, then data collected now might well lead to a slightly different model. This prediction applies only to the sons of fathers in the UK in the 1890s. Moreover, the families measured in Pearson's study were predominantly middle class, so the prediction applies to middle class families in the 1890s. (A different model might have been required for the heights of fathers and sons in working class families.)

(c) There is a lot of scatter in the plot, so any individual son of a 70-inch-tall man could be a lot taller or shorter than 69.9 inches. This height is an estimate of the mean height of sons of 70-inch-tall men in the UK in the 1890s.

Solution 2.3

(a) The scatterplot is shown in Figure S5.2.

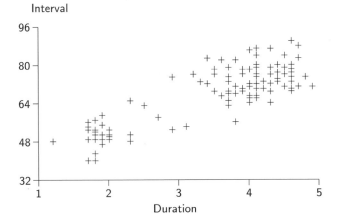

Figure S5.2 A scatterplot of time to next eruption against duration of eruption

(b) There seem to be two main groups of points on the scatterplot, corresponding to 'short' and 'long' eruptions. 'Short' eruptions lasted two minutes or less; 'long' eruptions lasted more than three minutes. Very few of the eruptions were of intermediate duration. However, overall, the time to the next eruption appears to increase with the length of the current eruption. Following a long eruption, there is a longer wait, on average, until the the next eruption than following a short eruption. However, there is a lot of scatter in the plot, so the relationship is not a very strong one. It does look as though a straight line might summarise the relationship quite well.

Solution 2.4

(a) The equation of the least squares fit line is

$$y = 33.65 + 9.806x,$$

where x minutes is the duration of an eruption and y minutes is the waiting time until the start of the next eruption.

(i) After an eruption of length 1.5 minutes, the predicted time until the start of the next eruption is

$$33.65 + 9.806 \times 1.5 \simeq 48.4 \text{ minutes}.$$

(ii) After an eruption of length 3 minutes, the predicted time until the start of the next eruption is

$$33.65 + 9.806 \times 3 \simeq 63.1 \text{ minutes}.$$

(iii) After an eruption of length 4.5 minutes, the predicted time until the start of the next eruption is

$$33.65 + 9.806 \times 4.5 \simeq 77.8 \text{ minutes}.$$

(b) The predictions are estimates of the *mean* waiting time until the next eruption following eruptions of lengths 1.5, 3 and 4.5 minutes, and

there is a lot of scatter about the regression line. So the next eruption may be much sooner or much later than predicted. Nevertheless, the predictions could be used to give a very rough indication of when the next eruption is likely to occur: the mean waiting time is nearly half an hour longer following a 4.5 minute eruption than following a 1.5 minute eruption. This is a situation where a confidence interval might be more useful than a simple prediction. The lower confidence limit might be useful as an indication of the earliest time that the next eruption is likely to occur.

Solution 2.5

(a) There is a lot of scatter in the plot, but it does look as though there might be a weak relationship between memorisation time and city block score. The equation of the least squares fit line is

$$y = 36.81 - 0.1793x,$$

where x is the memorisation time in seconds and y is the city block score.

(b) Again there is a lot of scatter in the plot, but less than in the scatterplot for the elderly group. The equation of the least squares fit line is

$$y = 32.61 - 0.1836x.$$

(c) The equation of the least squares fit line for the combined group is

$$y = 38.07 - 0.2264x.$$

According to this model, the predicted city block scores are as follows.

(i) When the memorisation time is 1 minute, the predicted score is

$$38.07 - 0.2264 \times 60 \simeq 24.$$

(ii) When the memorisation time is 2 minutes, the predicted score is

$$38.07 - 0.2264 \times 120 \simeq 11.$$

(iii) When the memorisation time is 3 minutes, the predicted score is

$$38.07 - 0.2264 \times 180 \simeq -3.$$

Clearly, a city block score of -3 is impossible; the lowest possible score is 0, for someone who replaces all the objects in the correct positions. Note that three minutes is outside the range of memorisation times for the people taking the test, so using the model for prediction is not valid in this case. Clearly, the model is not appropriate for times as long as three minutes. Since the lowest possible score is 0, a model which does not predict values below zero might be considered. Might a curve rather than a straight line provide a more useful model?

Solution 2.6

In order to draw the lines, I found the coordinates of two points on each line: $(25, 32.3)$ and $(150, 9.9)$ for the fit line for the elderly group; $(25, 28.0)$ and $(150, 5.1)$ for the fit line for the young group. The two least squares fit lines are drawn on the scatterplot in Figure S5.3.

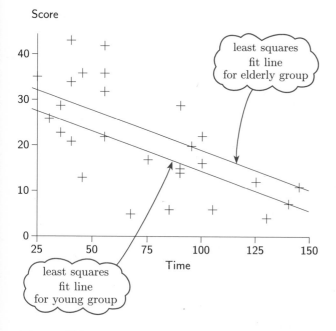

Figure S5.3   The two least squares fit lines

As you can see, the gradients of the two lines are roughly equal. However, the line for the elderly group is a little higher than the line for the young group, suggesting that elderly people do not perform quite as well as young people who spend similar times memorising the positions of the objects. Is there a real difference, or is the observed difference between the lines simply due to sampling variation? This is the sort of question that more advanced regression techniques can tackle. It is possible to fit parallel lines to two data sets and then to carry out a hypothesis test of whether there is a 'real' difference between the intercepts or whether the observed difference might be due to chance. However, we shall not be discussing how to do this in this course.

Chapter D5

Solution 3.2

The log–lin plot and the least squares fit line are shown in Figure S5.4. The line appears to provide a reasonable model for the pattern in the plot. None of the points is a long way from the line. (But notice that it looks as though the pattern might possibly be modelled better by a gently curving line.)

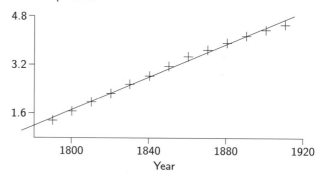

Figure S5.4   The log–lin plot and the least squares fit line

The equation of the least squares fit line is

$$y = -46.51 + 0.0268x,$$

where x is the year and y is LNPopulation, so

$$\text{LNPopulation} = -46.51 + 0.0268\,\text{Year},$$

or, replacing the capital letters LN of OUStats by the more usual ln,

$$\ln \text{Population} = -46.51 + 0.0268\,\text{Year}.$$

Solution 3.3

From

$$\ln \text{Population} = -46.51 + 0.0268\,\text{Year},$$

it follows that

$$
\begin{aligned}
\text{Population} &= \exp(-46.51 + 0.0268\,\text{Year}) \\
&= \exp(-46.51)\exp(0.0268\,\text{Year}) \\
&= 6.324 \times 10^{-21} \exp(0.0268\,\text{Year}).
\end{aligned}
$$

Solution 3.4

(a)   From Solution 3.3, we have

$$\text{Population} = 6.324 \times 10^{-21} \exp(0.0268\,\text{Year}),$$

where the population is in millions. To use this equation to estimate the US population in 1885, we must substitute Year $= 1885$. This gives

$$
\begin{aligned}
\text{Population} &= 6.324 \times 10^{-21} \exp(0.0268 \times 1885) \\
&= 55.04
\end{aligned}
$$

rounded to four significant figures. So, according to the model, the US population was approximately 55.04 million in 1885.

(b)   Substituting Year $= 1920$ in the equation of the curve gives

$$
\begin{aligned}
\text{Population} &= 6.324 \times 10^{-21} \exp(0.0268 \times 1920) \\
&= 140.6
\end{aligned}
$$

rounded to four significant figures. Thus, assuming the model for the US population remains valid after 1910, it leads to an estimate of 140.6 million for the US population in 1920.

Substituting Year $= 1950$ in the equation of the curve gives

$$\text{Population} = 6.324 \times 10^{-21} \exp(0.0268 \times 1950)$$
$$= 314.2$$

rounded to four significant figures. Thus, assuming the model for the US population remains valid after 1910, it leads to an estimate of 314.2 million for the US population in 1950.

In fact, according to the US Bureau of the Census, the population of the USA was 105.7 million in 1920 and 151.1 million in 1950. So the model overestimates the US population in 1920 by more than 30%, and it leads to an estimate for the US population in 1950 which is more than twice as large as the actual population. This indicates that the fitted model does not remain valid outside the period covered by the data. This example illustrates the danger of using extrapolation.

Data on the US population at ten-year intervals from 1790 to 1960 are contained in the file USPOP2.OUS. You might like to fit a curve to these data and compare it with the one obtained using data for 1790 up to 1910 that you have been using in this activity.

Solution 3.5

(a) A scatterplot of pressure against volume is shown in Figure S5.5. Clearly, the relationship between the variables is not linear.

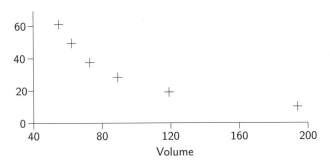

Figure S5.5 A scatterplot of the data

(b) If the relationship between P and V is of the form

$$PV^k = C,$$

then this is equivalent to

$$P = CV^{-k}.$$

This is a power law relationship, so a log–log plot should show a linear pattern.

Solution 3.6

(a) Figure S5.6 shows a scatterplot of LNPressure against LNVolume that I obtained using OUStats. The points lie approximately in a straight line.

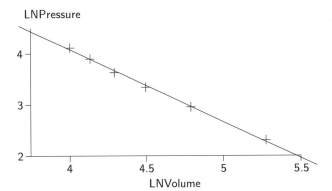

Figure S5.6 A log–log plot of the data

(b) The least squares fit line is also shown in Figure S5.6. As you can see, all the points lie very close to the line. The equation of the least squares fit line is

$$y = 9.679 - 1.404x,$$

where y is LNPressure and x is LNVolume. So

$$\text{LNPressure} = 9.679 - 1.404\text{LNVolume}.$$

(c) The equation can be written as

$$\ln \text{Pressure} = 9.679 + \ln(\text{Volume}^{-1.404})$$

(replacing LN by ln) or

$$\ln P = 9.679 + \ln(V^{-1.404}),$$

so

$$P = \exp(9.679 + \ln(V^{-1.404}))$$
$$= \exp(9.679)\exp(\ln(V^{-1.404}))$$
$$= 15\,980\,V^{-1.404},$$

rounding to 4 significant figures.

Hence the equation of a curve which models the relationship between the pressure and the volume of the gas is

$$P = 15\,980\,V^{-1.404}.$$

(d) The model predicts that, when the volume of the gas is 120 units, its pressure will be

$$P = 15\,980 \times 120^{-1.404} \simeq 19.2.$$

Solution 3.7

(a) A scatterplot of the data with the least squares fit line is shown in Figure S5.7.

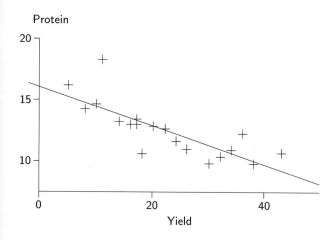

Figure **S5.7** A scatterplot of the data

A straight line does not provide a particularly good fit. As you can see, for intermediate values of the yield, all the points are on or below the fit line, whereas for several low values and for several high values, the points are above the line. This suggests that a curve might offer a better model for the relationship than a straight line.

(b) A log–lin plot and a log–log plot are shown in Figure S5.8 and Figure S5.9, respectively. (These plots were obtained using OUStats.)

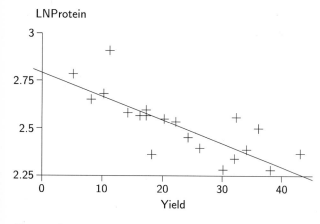

Figure **S5.8** A log–lin plot

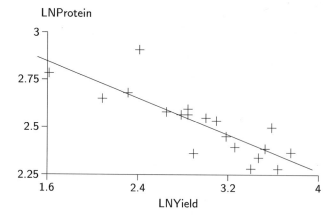

Figure **S5.9** A log–log plot

In the log–lin plot, all the points lie very close to or below the line for intermediate values of the yield, but above the line for several low and several high values. On the other hand, for the log–log plot the points are scattered either side of the least squares fit line across the whole range of values of lnYield. This suggests that a straight line is a better model for the pattern in the log–log plot than for the pattern in the log–lin plot.

Solution 3.8

(a) The equation of the least squares fit line for the log–log plot is

$$y = 3.234 - 0.2426x,$$

where $y = $ LNProtein and $x = $ LNYield. So (replacing LN by ln)

$$\ln \text{Protein} = 3.234 - 0.2426 \ln \text{Yield}$$
$$= 3.234 + \ln(\text{Yield}^{-0.2426}),$$

giving

$$\text{Protein} = \exp(3.234 + \ln(\text{Yield}^{-0.2426}))$$
$$= \exp(3.234)\exp(\ln(\text{Yield}^{-0.2426}))$$
$$= 25.38\,\text{Yield}^{-0.2426}.$$

(b) When the yield is 12.5 bushels per acre, the estimated percentage protein content of wheat is given by

$$\text{Protein} = 25.38 \times (12.5)^{-0.2426} \simeq 13.75.$$

Index for OUStats

Acknowledgements

Grateful acknowledgement is made to the following sources for permission to reproduce material in this book and on the Block D disk.

Draper, N. R. and Smith, H. (1966), *Applied Regression Analysis*, reprinted by permission of John Wiley and Sons, Inc. All rights reserved.

Fowler, J. and Cohen, L. (1996), *Statistics for Ornithologists, BTO Guide 22*, Second Edition, British Trust for Ornithology.

Reprinted with permission from Johnson, M. P. and Raven, P. H. (1973), 'Species number and endemism: the Galápagos Archipelago revisited', *Science*, **179**, pp. 893–895, Copyright © 1973 American Association for the Advancement of Science.

Lindgren, B. W. and Berry, D. A. (1981), *Elementary Statistics*, Macmillan Publishing Co., Inc., by permission of Prentice-Hall, Inc.

Mazess, R. B., Peppler, W. W. and Gibbons, M. (1984), 'Total body composition by dual-photon (^{153}Gd) absorptiometry', *American Journal of Clinical Nutrition*, **40**, pp. 834–839.

Metzger, W. H. (1935), *Journal of the American Society of Agronomy*, **27**, p. 653, American Society of Agronomy.

Selvin, S. (1991), *Statistical Analysis of Epidemiological Data*, New York, Oxford University Press.

Snedecor, G. W. and Cochran, W. G. (1980), *Statistical Methods*, Seventh Edition, The Iowa State University Press.

Sokal, R. R. and Rohlf, F. J. (1981), *Biometry*, Second Edition, W. H. Freeman and Company Publishers.

Spiegel, M. R. (1972), *Schaum's Outline of Theory and Problems of Statistics in SI Units*, reproduced with permission of The McGraw-Hill Companies.

Terman, L. M. 1919, *The Intelligence of School Children*, Copyright © 1919 by Houghton Mifflin Company. Renewed 1946. Reprinted with the permission of the author's estate.

Trumple, R. J. and Weaver, H. F. (1953), *Statistical Astronomy*, p. 194, Table 1.5, Copyright © 1953 The Regents of the University of California.

Wetherill, G. B. (1981), *Intermediate Statistical Methods*, Chapman and Hall.